The Story of the First Trans-Continental Railroad

W. F. Bailey

Contents

Preface 7
CHAPTER I. The Project and the Projectors. 11
CHAPTER II. The Proposition in Congress. 18
CHAPTER III. Mostly Financial. 24
CHAPTER IV. Commencement of the work. 31
CHAPTER V. Progress Made. 36
CHAPTER VI. Indian Troubles during construction. 46
CHAPTER VII. The Builders. 54
CHAPTER VIII. Completion of the Line. 62
CHAPTER IX. The Kansas Division (Kansas Pacific Railway.) *70*
CHAPTER X. The Denver-Cheyenne Line (Denver Pacific Railroad.) *79*
CHAPTER XI. History of the Line since its completion. 83
CHAPTER XII. The Central Pacific Railroad. 89

THE STORY OF THE FIRST TRANS-CONTINENTAL RAILROAD

BY

W. F. Bailey

Preface

For some reason the people of today are not nearly as familiar with the achievements of the last fifty years as they are with those of earlier days. The school boy can glibly recount the story of Columbus, William Penn, or Washington, but asked about the events leading up to the settlement of the West will know nothing of them and will probably reply "they don't teach us that in our school"--and it is true. Outside of the names of our presidents, the Rebellion, and the Spanish-American War, there is practically nothing of the events of the last fifty years in our school histories, and this is certainly wrong. "Peace hath her victories as well as War," and it is to the end that one of the great achievements of the last century may become better known that this account of the first great Pacific Railroad was written.

It was just as great an event for Lewis and Clark to cross the Rockies as it was for Columbus to cross the Atlantic. The Mormons not only made friends with the Indians as did Penn, but they also "made the desert to blossom as the rose," and Washington's battles at Princeton, White Plains, and Yorktown were but little more momentus in their results than Sandy Forsythe's on the Republican, Custer's on the Washita, or Crook's in the Sierra Madre.

The construction of the Union Pacific Railroad was of greater importance to the people of the United States than the inauguration of steamship service across the Atlantic or the laying of the Atlantic Telegraph. Yet the one has been heralded from time to time and the other allowed to sink into temporary obscurity.

To make good Americans of the coming generation all that is necessary is to make them proud of American achievements and the West was and is a field full of such.

The building of the Pacific Railroad was one of the great works of man. Its promoters were men of small means and little or no financial backing outside of the aid granted them by the Government. It took nerve and good Yankee grit to undertake and carry out the project. How it was done it is hoped the succeeding pages may show.

Fair Oaks, California, 1906.

Poem read at the Celebration of the opening of the Pacific Railroad, Chicago, May 10th, 1869.

Ring out, oh bells. Let cannons roar
  In loudest tones of thunder.
The iron bars from shore to shore
  Are laid and Nations wonder.

Through deserts vast and forests deep
  Through mountains grand and hoary
A path is opened for all time
  And we behold the glory.

We, who but yesterday appeared
  But settlers on the border,
Where only savages were reared
  Mid chaos and disorder.
We wake to find ourselves midway
  In continental station,
And send our greetings either way
  Across the mighty nation.

We reach out towards the golden gate
  And eastward to the ocean.
The tea will come at lightning rate
  And likewise Yankee notions.
From spicy islands off the West
  The breezes now are blowing,
And all creation does its best
  To set the greenbacks flowing.

The eastern tourist will turn out
  And visit all the stations
For Pullman runs upon the route
  With most attractive rations.

-- From the Chicago Tribune, May 11th, 1869.

CHAPTER I.
The Project and the Projectors.

President Jefferson First to Act on a Route to the Pacific--Lewis and Clark Expedition--Oregon Missionaries--Railroad Suggested--Mills 1819--The Emigrant 1832--Parker 1835--Dr. Barlow's Plan--Hartwell Carver's--John Plumbe's--Asa Whitney--Senator Benton's National Road.

It would appear that Thomas Jefferson is entitled to the credit of being the first to take action towards the opening of a road or route between the eastern states and the Pacific Coast. While he was in France in 1779 as American Envoy to the Court of Versailles he met one John Ledyard who had been with Captain Cook in his voyage around the world, in the course of which they had visited the coast of California. Out of the acquaintance grew an expedition under Ledyard that was to cross Russia and the Pacific Ocean to Alaska, thence take a Russian trading vessel from Sitka to the Spanish-Russian settlement on Nookta Sound (Coast of California) and from there proceed east overland until the settlements then confined to the Atlantic Seaboard were reached.

Through the efforts of Jefferson the expedition was equipped and started. The Russian Government had promised its support but when the party had crossed Russia, were within two hundred miles of the Pacific, Ledyard was arrested by order of the Empress Catherine, the then ruler of Russia, and the expedition broken up.

Jefferson became President in 1801. In 1803 on his recommendation, Congress made an appropriation "for sending an exploring party to trace the Missouri River to its source, to cross the highlands (i. e. Rocky Mountains) and follow the best route thence to the Pacific Ocean."

So interested was Jefferson that he personally prepared a long and specific letter of instructions and had his confidential man placed in charge. "The object of your mission," said Jefferson, in this letter of instruction "is to explore the Missouri River and such other streams as by their course would seem to offer the most direct and practicable communication across the continent for the purpose of commerce." This expedition known as the Lewis and Clark, made in 1804-1806, brought to light much information relative to the West and demonstrated conclusively the feasibility of crossing overland as well as the resources of the country traversed.

As a result the far West became the Mecca of the fur trappers and traders. Commencing with the Astoria settlement in 1807, for the next forty years or until the opening of the Oregon immigration in 1844, they were practically the only whites to visit it outside of the missionaries, who did more or less exploring and visiting the Indians resulting in the Rev. Jason Lee in 1833 and Dr. Marcus Whitman in 1835 having established mission stations in Oregon.

The next record is of one Robert Mills of Virginia who suggested in a publication on "Internal Improvements in Maryland, Virginia, and South Carolina," issued in 1819, the advisability of connecting the head of navigation of some one of the principal streams entering the Atlantic with the Pacific Ocean by a system of steam propelled carriages. (H. R. Doc. 173, 29th Cong.) This was before there was a mile of Steam Railroad in the world, and under the then existing circumstances was so chimerical as to hardly warrant mention.

In a weekly newspaper published in 1832 at Ann Arbor, Michigan, called "The Emigrant," appeared what was probably the first suggestion in print on the advisability of a Pacific Railroad. The article suggests the advisability of building a line from New York to the Mouth of the Oregon (Columbia River) by way of the south shore of Lake Erie and Lake Michigan, crossing the Mississippi River between 41 and 42 north latitude, the Missouri River about the mouth of the Platte, thence to the Rocky Mountains near the source of the last named river, crossing them and down the valley of the Oregon to the Pacific. It further suggested that it be made a national project, or this failing the grant of three millions of acres to a Company organized for the purpose of constructing it. No name was signed to the article, but the probabilities are that it was written by S. W. Dexter, the Editor of the paper.

With the Whitman party leaving the East for the far northwest to establish a Mission Station was the Rev. Samuel Parker, a Presbyterian minister, who was sent under the auspices of the Missionary Board of his Church to investigate and report on the mission situation and to suggest a plan for Christianizing the Indians. He crossed the continent to Oregon and on his return in 1838, his journal was published. It presented a very correct and interesting account of the scenes he visited. In it he says, "There would be no difficulty in the way of constructing a railroad from the Atlantic to the Pacific Ocean * * * * and the time may not be so far distant when trips will be made across the continent as they are now to Niagara Falls to see Nature's wonders."

To just whom belongs the credit of being the first to advocate a railroad to the Pacific Coast is in dispute. No doubt the idea occurred to many at the time they were being introduced and successfully operated in the East. The two items referred to seem to be the first record of the idea or possibility.

About the same time, although the date is not positively fixed, Dr. Samuel Bancroft Barlow, a practising physician of Greenville, Mass., commenced writing articles for the newspapers, advocating a Pacific railroad and outlining a plan for its construction.

His proposition contemplated a railroad from New York City to the mouth of the Columbia River. As illustrating the lack of knowledge regarding the cost and operations of railroads, we quote from his writings "Premising the length of the road would be three thousand miles and the average cost ten thousand dollars per mile, we have thirty million dollars as the total cost, and were the United States to engage in its construction, three years time would be amply sufficient * * * * At the very moderate rate of ten miles an hour, a man could go from New York to the mouth of the Columbia River in twelve days and a half."

Another enthusiast was Hartwell Carver, grandson of Jonathan Carver the explorer of 1766. His proposition was to build a railroad from Lake Michigan (Chicago) to the South Pass, with two branches from there, one to the mouth of the Columbia River, and the other due west to California. South Pass received its name from being South of the pass in general use. Strange to say his "true Pacific Route" formulated without knowledge of the lay of the land was absolutely the best and the one that today is followed by the Union Pacific Railway and affiliated lines, substituting Granger for South Pass. Carver's proposition was to build the line by a private corporation who were to receive a grant of land for their right of way, the whole distance, with the privilege of taking from the public lands, material used in construction, with the further privilege of purchasing from the United States Government, eight million acres of selected lands from the public domains at one dollar and twenty-five cents per acre, payable in the stock of the Company. His road was to be laid on stone foundations and to be equipped with sleeping cars, dining cars and salon cars. His ideas as to the cost of the work were far too low, but outside of this he was seemingly inspired. At the time he was writing, 1835, there were seven hundred and ninety-seven miles of railroads in operation in the United States. Passenger coaches were patterned after the old stage coach, the track iron straps on wooden stringers, yet here he was outlining what today is an accomplished fact. A railroad with stone ballast from Chicago to the South Pass (Granger, Wyo.) one branch diverging from there to the mouth of the Columbia, (Portland, Ore.,) the other to California, (San Francisco and Los Angeles, Cal.,) traversed by trains comprised of sleeping cars, dining cars and buffet cars. The Union Pacific and its connections.

Carver spent the best years of his life and what was in those days an ample fortune in endeavoring to further his project. The great opposition to his plan arose from the proposed diversion of the public lands and the stock feature, neither Congress nor the public taking kindly to the idea of the Government giving lands for stock in a private corporation.

A third proposition was fathered by John Plumbe of Dubuque, Iowa, who suggested at a public meeting, held at his home town in March 1838, that a railroad be built from the great lakes to the Columbia River. His plan contemplated an appropriation from Congress of alternate sections of the public lands on either side of the right of way. The company to be capitalized at one hundred million dollars, twenty million shares at five dollars each. Twenty-five cents per share to be paid down to provide a fund to commence operations and subsequent assessments of like amount to be paid as the money was needed until the full amount had been paid in. One hundred miles to be constructed each year and the whole line completed in twenty years.

All of these propositions were more or less visionary and advanced by men of theory with little or no capital. They had the effect of awakening public interest and paved the way for a more feasible plan. The question of a Pacific railway, its practicability, earnings, and effect, were constantly before the people. In 1844 the idea had become firmly fixed, the leading advocate being a New York merchant named Asa Whitney, who has been called the "Father of the Pacific Railway." Mr. Whitney had spent some years in commercial life in China, returning to the United States with a competency. Becoming enthused with the idea, he put his all,--energy, time, and money into the project of a trans-continental railroad, finding many supporters. At first he advocated Carver's plan, but becoming convinced that it was not feasible, he sprung a new one of his own. He proposed that Congress should give to him, his heirs and assigns, a strip of land, sixty miles wide, with the railroad in the center, this from a point on Lake Michigan to the Pacific Coast. This land he proposed to colonize and sell to emigrants from Europe, from the proceeds build the line, retaining whatever surplus there might be after its completion, as his own.

Whitney was an indefatigable worker, thoroughly in earnest, a fluent speaker, both in public and private, well fortified with statistics and arguments. He personally travelled the whole country from Maine to fifteen miles up the Missouri River. The legislatures of Maine, New Hampshire, Vermont, Rhode Island, New Jersey, Connecticut, New York, Maryland, Ohio, Indiana, Illinois, Michigan, Tennessee, Alabama, and Georgia, all endorsed his plan by favorable resolutions.

The Senate Committee on public lands made a report recommending his proposition. Thus strongly endorsed, his plan was brought before Congress in 1848 in a bill entitled "Authorizing Asa Whitney, his heirs or assigns, to construct a railroad from any point on Lake Michigan or the Mississippi River he may designate, in a line as nearly straight as practicable, to some point on the Pacific Ocean where a harbor may be had." The road to be six foot gauge, sixty-four pound rails. The Government to establish tolls and regulate the operation of the line, Whitney to be the sole Owner and receive a salary of four thousand dollars per year for managing it.

The proposition was debated for days in the Senate and then was tabled on a vote of twenty-seven to twenty-one. The opposition dwelt largely on the length of time Whitney would necessarily require. Say he could colonize and sell a million acres a year, this would only be funds enough to build one hundred miles and consequently the two thousand miles would require at least twenty years. The defeat was largely owing to the opposition of Senator Benton of Missouri, the most pronounced friend of the West in the House, who used the argument of the power and capital it would put in the hands of one man, Whitney's. This he characterized as a project to give away an Empire, larger in extent than eight of the original states, with an ocean frontage of sixty miles, with contracting powers and patronage exceeding those of the President.

Upon the defeat of Whitney's project, Benton brought forward in 1849 one of his own for a great national highway from St. Louis to San Francisco, straight as may be, with branches to Oregon and Mexico. The Government to grant a strip one mile wide, so as to provide room for every kind of road, railway, plank, macadamized, and electric motor, or otherwise constructed where not so practicable or advantageous. Sleighs to be used during those months when snow lay on the ground. Funds for its construction to be provided by the sale of public lands. Bare in mind this was only fifty-six years ago, but eighteen years before the Union Pacific Railway was completed, and was the proposition advocated by the recognized leader of the Senate in matters western.

Up to the year 1846 when by the treaty of Guadeloupe-Hidalgo, Mexico, ceded to us California, our only territory on the Pacific Coast was Oregon and Washington. The acquisition of California, followed very shortly by the gold discoveries and the consequent influx of people, gave that state a large population and furnished a prospective business for a Pacific railway. This had heretofore been a matter of theory, very questionable, to say the least, being based on very hazy estimates of the prospective volume of trans-pacific business. With an active and aggressive population of three hundred thousand in California, practically all of eastern birth and affiliations the situation became materially changed and the necessity of railroad communication apparent. Both great political parties pledged their support in their quadrennial platforms. Presidents--Pierce, Buchanan, and Lincoln, in their several messages to Congress, strongly recommended its construction. The matter had been thoroughly discussed, both in and out of Congress and the whole country was convinced of the advisability of its construction, and only awaited a leader and a feasible plan. From 1850 to 1860 the question vied with that of slavery in public interest. Survey after survey was undertaken by the Government and private parties. Senator Benton being the first to introduce a resolution looking to the appropriation of sufficient money to pay for a survey. This being in 1851. The question of the North and South, entered into the matter, as it did everything else in the days preceding the Rebellion. "You shall not build through free soil," said the South and "we won't permit it to run through the Slave States," said the North. Compromise was out of the question, and it was not until the southern element had been eliminated from Congress by their secession was any action possible.

It was found that private corporations, duly aided by land grants from the Government, were able to build the necessary connecting links through the comparatively level country, between Chicago and St. Louis, and the Missouri River. From the Missouri River west it was felt that the undertaking was too great for any one set of men or corporation, besides local interests in California were already in the field, consequently two companies were determined upon, one of them working eastward, the other westward, and it was thus arranged.

CHAPTER II.
The Proposition in Congress.

Situation 1861--Curtis Bill of 1862--Amended Charter of 1864--Further Amendments--1866--Legal Complications in New York--Controversy With Central Pacific.

Commencing with the session of 1835, when a memorial on the subject of railroad communication between Lake Michigan and the Pacific Coast, was presented by Hartwell Carver, up to the present, the Pacific Railways have been ever present in Congress. The Catalogue of Government Publications gives one hundred and eighty-five having the Union Pacific, or Pacific Railroads as their subject.

It is not necessary to recount the many schemes for the construction of these roads that were proposed to Congress. We have already outlined the principal ones previous to 1861.

At this time our country was in the midst of its greatest difficulties. The North and South unable to harmonize over the slavery question, had recourse to the arbitration of arms. The Union forces had met with numerous and severe reverses. The people of the Pacific Coast were loud in their demands for better means of communication. The Government was straining to what seemed the breaking point, their credit and resources to carry on the war and as a Government enterprise the building of a Pacific Railway was out of the question. All were convinced of not only the desirability of such a line but of the absolute necessity thereof, and it had resolved itself into a question of ways and means. Previous discussions had thrashed out the chaff and it now remained for Congress to winnow the wheat. Government surveys had demonstrated the existence of five feasible routes through or over the

Rocky Mountains. The Northern, now followed by the Northern Pacific Railroad, the South Pass, Snake and Columbia Rivers, now traversed by the Union Pacific Railroad to Granger, thence the Oregon Short Line and Oregon Railway and Navigation Company. The Middle Route-Union Pacific Railroad in connection with the Southern Pacific Company (Central Pacific Railroad). The thirty-ninth parallel route, now followed by the Santa Fe Route and the Southern via El Paso, now followed by the Sunset Route. The first two while available, could be eliminated owing to their not reaching California direct, as could also the two latter, on account of their traversing in part at least, country that was then in a state of insurrection.

These reasons were in themselves sufficient to determine the selection, but with the many other arguments advanced, there was no trouble in bringing Congress to adopt practically unanimously the "South Pass" "Middle" "True Pacific" Route as it was variously called. For years this had been the route of the fur traders and trappers, the emigrant, the Overland Stage, and the Pony Express, and if these various interests had agreed as to this being the shortest and best route it was evident there were good and sufficient reasons for their decision, it being incontrovertible that it was the shortest one that reached the desired territory. Especially as their decision was reinforced by the result of numerous surveys made by the Government.

The bill creating the Union Pacific Railroad was known as the "Curtis Bill" from its author, Congressman S. R. Curtis of Iowa. It carried the title of "An Act to aid in the construction of a railroad and telegraph line from the Missouri River to the Pacific Ocean and to secure to the United States Government, the use thereof for postal, military, and other purposes."

This act passed the Senate, June 20th, 1862, by a vote of thirty-five to two and became a law July 1st, of that same year. In addition to creating the Union Pacific Railroad Company it also authorized the Central Pacific Railroad Company to build a railroad from Sacramento to the eastern boundary of California, where it was to connect with the Union Pacific Railroad. The bill also recognized a Company chartered by the legislature of Kansas under the name of the Leavenworth, Pawnee and Western Railway Company, later known as the Kansas Pacific Railway. This latter line was to be built from Leavenworth west to a junction with the Union Pacific Railroad at or near the hundredth Meridian or about two hundred and fifty miles west of Omaha.

The principal features of the bill so far as the Union Pacific Railroad were concerned, were, the creation of a Board of Commissioners consisting of one hundred and fifty-eight commissioners to represent the interest of the United States Government and who were to be named by the Secretary of the Interior. These were to constitute a preliminary organization.

The Union Pacific Railroad proper was to commence at a point on the hundredth Meridian, west of Greenwich, between the Valley of the Platte River on the north and the Valley on the Republican River on the south, with branch lines to be known as the Iowa Branch from said point to the Missouri River. On the west it was to extend to the Eastern boundary of California, where it was to connect with the Central Pacific Railroad.

The Capital stock of the Company was to consist of ten thousand shares at one thousand dollars each, not more than two hundred shares to be held by any one person. Right of way through public lands was granted with the privilege of taking therefrom, without charge, earth, stone, lumber, or other material for construction purposes. The Company was granted every alternate section of land as designated by odd numbers to the amount of five sections per mile, on each side of the road within the limits of ten miles, not sold, reserved or otherwise disposed of by the Government, and to which a pre-emption or homestead claim had not been made up to the time the road was finally located, mineral lands being excepted. All lands thus granted, not sold or disposed of three years after the line was completed, were to be sold by the Government at not to exceed one dollar and twenty-five cents per acre, the proceeds to accrue to the Railroad Company. Nothing but American iron was to be used in the rails. As fast as sections of forty miles were completed and accepted by commissioners appointed by the Government for that purpose, one thousand dollar bonds of the United States bearing six per cent. interest, payable in thirty years, were to be issued to the Company constructing the line. Sixteen thousand dollars in bonds to the mile for the distance east of the Rocky Mountains and forty-eight thousand to the mile for one hundred and fifty miles for the mountain portion of the line. Three-fourths of these bonds were to be delivered to the railroad Company as the sections were accepted, the remaining fourth to be retained by the Government until the entire line was completed. The bonds to constitute a first mortgage on the entire line equipment, terminals, etc? The road to be completed within twelve years, the first one hundred miles within two years. Five per cent. of the net earnings, together with the entire amount accruing on transportation furnished the Government was to be applied to the payment of these bonds, principal and interest.

The Bill which in reality constituted a Charter, also provided that the gauge of the road and its eastern terminus should be left to the President of the United States to determine.

These somewhat onerous conditions were accepted by the promoters. Subscription books opened but capital fought shy of the proposition. Two years solicitation only resulted in subscriptions to the amount of two million dollars being paid up in cash.

It being evident that the necessary funds could not be procured on the terms of the original act, an appeal was made to Congress resulting in a supplementary act passing the House of Representatives, July 2nd, 1864, and soon thereafter becoming law. This increased the amount of the Land Grant to the odd numbered sections within ten miles of either side the track, and made the bonds of the Government a second mortgage instead of first, they to be issued on sections of twenty miles instead of forty, two-thirds of the bonds being available as soon as the grading was done. The limit extended in which the line must be completed, and but one-half the earnings on Government business withheld to meet the bonds. The Company was also authorized to maintain a ferry or ferries across the Missouri River at Omaha as a means of connection with the Iowa Lines until such time as they could construct a bridge suitable for this purpose. Coupled with these favorable amendments were two provisions that eventually militated against the Company. One of them permitting the Kansas Pacific Railway to connect with the Union Pacific Railroad at any point its projectors saw fit at or east of a point fifty miles west of Denver, Colo., instead of at the hundredth Meridian. This created a competitor instead of a feeder. The second was allowing the Central Pacific Railroad Company to build on east one hundred and fifty miles to meet the road from the East instead of stopping at the California State line. The restriction to one hundred and fifty miles was withdrawn in subsequent legislation. This resulted in a race as to which Company should cover the most ground and involved both of them in much additional expense. With the Charter thus amended, the Union Pacific Railroad Company which had not thus far done any real work, commenced active construction. The Credit Mobilier was formed to do the actual building, and with many trials, discouragements, and unforeseen expense, the work was continued to its completion.

The initial eastern point had been fixed by the Charter two hundred and forty-seven miles west of Omaha--at the hundredth Meridian, branches being contemplated to connect it with the Missouri River. In 1866 Congress authorized commencement at Omaha without reference to this fact,--the line to extend from Omaha to a connection with the Central Pacific Railroad.

The question of the gauge or width of track was another matter that occupied the attention of Congress. The question had by the Charter been left to the President. There was a divergence of opinions as to the best gauge for railroad tracks. At this time the Erie, and Ohio and Mississippi Railroads used a six foot gauge. The California legislature had fixed five foot as the gauge in that state, while the principal eastern roads including the Baltimore and Ohio, New York Central as well as the Chicago and Iowa lines, were what is known as standard gauge (i. e. four feet, eight and a half inches.) A committee of Parliament had settled on five feet, three inches as the gauge in England. President Lincoln had announced himself as in favor of five foot and the Central Pacific people had ordered their equipment of that width. The influence of the Chicago-Iowa lines as well as that of the Union Pacific people, was thrown in favor of the so called standard gauge, and on March 2nd, 1863, Congress passed what is one of the shortest laws on the Statute Books, namely,

"Be it enacted by the Senate and House of Representatives of   the United States in Congress assembled, that the gauge of   the Pacific Railroad and its branches through its whole   extent from the Pacific Coast to the Missouri River, shall   be and hereby is established at four feet, eight and   one-half inches."

In 1869 about the time the Credit Mobilier Company was about to turn the finished road over, disgruntled stock and bondholders under the leadership of "Jim Fisk" endeavored to wrest possession from the Union Pacific Railway Company. Certain stock was recorded in his name and although paid for with a check that was refused by the bank on which it was drawn, Fisk went into court and secured an injunction preventing the board of directors acting until his relations with the Company had been adjudicated by the Courts. Under cover of these legal proceedings in the state courts, the New York Offices were forcibly entered, the books and securities of the Company removed and a feeling of insecurity and uncertainty aroused that caused a serious depreciation in the value of the securities they were endeavoring to market. W. M. Tweede being appointed receiver by the State Courts of such property of the Company as was to be found within its jurisdiction. It is said the trouble cost the Company some six or seven million dollars. Appealing to Congress, they were granted authority to remove its eastern offices from New York City to Boston. The next appearance in Congress was made necessary by a dispute with the Central Pacific Company over the point of connection. The Union Pacific Company claimed their grade extended to Humboldt Wells, five hundred miles west of Ogden, while the Central Pacific in reprisal claimed the line to the western end of Weber Canon some thirty miles east of Ogden. The facts were the two completed lines met at Promontory Point fifty-three miles west of Ogden, April 28th, 1869. By act of Congress, it was decided that the Union Pacific Railroad Company should build the line to Promontory where the two roads should connect but that the Central Pacific Railroad Company should pay for and own the line west of Ogden. This was "settled out of Court" and the action of Congress simply ratified an agreement made by the two Companies.

The above covers the more important matters so far as the action of Congress was concerned. Many other minor matters received attention at their hands--both before and since the completion of the road. As is stated in the opening paragraph of this chapter, the Pacific Railroads have been ever present in Congress. The more important questions being referred to in their order later.

CHAPTER III.
Mostly Financial.

Preliminary Organization--Board of Commissioners--Company Organized--Directors and Officers Elected--Hoxie Contract--Credit Mobilier--Ames' Interest--Compromise Contract--Davis Contract--Cost of Line--Land Grant.

When the Pacific Railroad Bill passed Congress and received the President's signature in 1862, there was a well organized company to take hold of the western or California end. The Union Pacific or eastern end was not in such good shape. Thomas C. Durant, who was afterwards Vice President of the Company had with a few associates taken a prominent part in the matter but no regular organization existed.

Under the Charter there were one hundred and fifty-eight persons named, who, together with five to be appointed by the Secretary of the Interior were to constitute a "Board of Commissioners" to effect a preliminary organization, open books for the subscription of stock and to call a meeting of the stockholders to elect a board of directors as soon as two thousand shares had been subscribed and ten dollars per share paid in.

When the board of directors had been elected, the property or rather the proposition was to be turned over to them and the duties of the Board of Commissioners should cease and terminate.

The Company thus organized, should follow established precedents, stockholders should hold annual meetings, elect a board of directors, and adopt bylaws and rules for the conduct of its affairs. The directors thus elected to be not less than thirteen in number, two to be added to their number by appointment of the President of the United States. The Board of Directors to elect the officers of the company and exercise supervision.

The Board of Commissioners met in Chicago in September, 1862, and organized, electing W. B. Ogden, President and H. V. Poor, Secretary, as called for in the charter, and subscription books were duly opened. There was no disposition on the part of moneyed men to subscribe for the stock and it was only owing to a few public-spirited men coming in and taking the two thousand shares that the Charter did not lapse. When the necessary stock had been subscribed, a meeting of the stockholders was held in New York City, in October, 1863, at which a Board of Directors were to be elected,--a strange situation confronted them, there being no man or set of men who were able to assume control, although there were no lack of cliques who were desirous of doing so, but these were largely irresponsible parties either lacking in the necessary capital or not command the confidence of those who did have it.

Something had to be done, and accordingly thirty men of more or less prominence were elected to the position of directors, some of them without their knowledge and some declined to serve. The Company was accordingly organized October 30th, 1863. General John A. Dix, who was elected President, had been a member of the Cabinet and later a general in the United States Army, was a man who was universally respected. The position was not of his seeking, and he gave notice he had neither the time nor inclination to give active attention to its affairs and the burden was practically assumed by the Vice-President Elect, Thomas C. Durant. But two hundred and eighteen thousand dollars the ten dollars per share called for by the Charter on two thousand one hundred and eighty shares had been paid in and further funds were not obtainable. Agitation was kept up and due representation made to Congress, resulting in an amendment to the Charter being passed. After the passage of the Supplementary Act in 1864 made necessary by the failure to secure funds, it was still regarded as an unpromising investment for the reason that investors could not feel any assurance that they or their friends would have any voice in the management of affairs or control of the Company. The capital of the Company was fixed by the supplementary act at one hundred million dollars, (one million shares at one hundred dollars each), consequently any interest holding over fifty millions of the stock would be paramount and vice versa. Until it was determined who would be in control, investors fought shy. Under the Charter the subscription books must remain open until the completion of the road, making it possible for outsiders to wait until the road was near completion and then step in and by large subscriptions acquire control.

As there were some funds available, a contract was entered into in May, 1864, with H. M. Hoxie, to build the first hundred miles. This contract was extended to cover from Omaha to the hundredth Meridian, two hundred and forty-seven miles, on October 3rd, 1864, and on the 7th of the same month assigned to a company (simple partnership) composed of Vice-President Durant and six others, all stockholders of the Railroad Company. The capital of this partnership consisted of four hundred thousand dollars (but a small percentage of the amount necessary to carry out the Hoxie contract). The members of the firm were unable or else unwilling, owing to the immense personal liability involved, to put up further funds and some other action was necessary.

Durant and his friends accordingly purchased the Charter of a Pennsylvania Corporation of limited liability and elastic powers, known as the "Pennsylvania Fiscal Agency" changed its name by legislative enactment to the Credit Mobilier of America. Subscribers of the two million one hundred and eighty thousand dollars of Union Pacific Stock were given the option of either exchanging Union Pacific stock for that of the Credit Mobilier, sell their Union Pacific stock to the Credit Mobilier, or turn it back to the Union Pacific Railroad Company and have it redeemed. By this the stockholders of the Credit Mobilier became the sole holders of the Union Pacific stock.

The Hoxie contract was reassigned to the Credit Mobilier who duly completed the work, finishing the line to the point specified October 5th, 1866. Owing to their inability to raise funds, it seemed as though the two companies, Union Pacific and Credit Mobilier, would fall down. There was no sale for the First Mortgage bonds of the railroad, the Government bonds were but little better, being worth but sixty-five cents on the dollar. Durant and his friends were not men of wealth nor did they command the confidence of wealthy men. The Company had become greatly involved and was compelled to sell some of its rolling stock to pay pressing debts. It was at this junction that Oakes Ames entered the field, being persuaded, it is said, to do so by President Lincoln who desired to enlist his well-known executive ability and capital in the enterprise. Through the efforts of himself and associates the paid up subscriptions were increased to two and a half million dollars.

The original or first contract made with Hoxie for a hundred miles had been extended to cover up to the hundredth Meridian, and the line to that point, two hundred and forty-seven miles from Omaha, was completed October 5th, 1866.

The second contract made was with a Mr. Boomer for one hundred and fifty-three and thirty-five hundredths miles from the hundredth Meridian west, at the rate of nineteen thousand five hundred dollars per mile for that part of the distance East of the North Platte River and twenty thousand dollars per mile west thereof. Bridges, station buildings, and equipment to be additional. This contract was also assigned to the Credit Mobilier. On this, fifty-eight miles were completed when dissensions arose, occasioned by financial stringency among the stockholders of the Credit Mobilier. Vice-President Durant going into court, compelled suspension of action on the third contract, made March 1st, 1867, with one J. M. Williams who had assigned it to the Credit Mobilier. This covered two hundred and sixty-six and fifty-two hundredths miles, commencing at the hundredth Meridian at the rate of fifty thousand dollars per mile. For a time matters were at a standstill, injunctions preventing the completion of present or the making of new contracts.

Finally a compromise was affected between the two factions, Durant and his friends on the one side, and the Ames interests on the other.

Under this, a fourth contract was made with Oakes Ames for which he was to receive from forty-two thousand to ninety-six thousand dollars per mile or forty-seven million nine hundred and fifteen thousand dollars for six hundred and sixty-seven miles, commencing at the hundredth Meridian. This it is supposed is the largest contract ever made by one individual. It was later transferred by Oakes Ames to seven trustees acting for the Credit Mobilier, he and his brother Oliver Ames being among the number. This last contract carried the line to nine hundred and fourteen miles from Omaha.

The fifth contract was made with J. W. Davis for one hundred and twenty-two miles at twenty-three million four hundred thousand dollars, and was in turn assigned to the same seven trustees for completion. In adjustment of accounts the Union Pacific Railroad Company would turn over to the Credit Mobilier or the Trustees for the Credit Mobilier in payment for the work as fast as it was completed

First Mortgage (Union Pacific Railroad) Bonds, Government Bonds, Union Pacific Railroad Income Bonds and Union Pacific Railroad Stock, these being sold or hypothecated by the trustees, furnished them the necessary funds required to pay for the construction work.

As the Union Pacific Stock could only be sold for cash at par according to act of Congress, notwithstanding it was only worth thirty cents on the market, the Railroad Company would give their check to the Credit Mobilier on construction account and this check could then be used in payment of stock, making it a cash transaction.

In settlement of the several contracts, the Union Pacific Railroad Company paid the Credit Mobilier:

	Miles	
Hoxie Contract		
Omaha to 100th Meridian	247	$12,974,416.24
Ames Contract		
100th Meridian West	667	57,140,102.94
Davis Contract		
To point five miles west of Ogden	125	23,431,768.10
	1039	$93,546,287.28

These figures represent stocks and bonds at par and deducting amount of depreciation, would bring the actual cost of the Main Line Omaha to Ogden to about seventy-three million dollars.

There were issued in payment for this construction, equipment, station building, and the expense of the Company during the construction period.

Government Bonds	$ 27,236,512.00
First Mortgage Bonds	27,213,000.00
Income Bonds	9,355,000.00
Land Grant Bonds	9,224,000.00
Union Pacific Stock	36,000,000.00
	$109,028,512.00

There were granted to the Union Pacific Railroad Company under its Charter land grants of eleven million three hundred and nine thousand eight hundred and forty-four acres. Up to December 31st, 1866, sales of this land had brought in nineteen million ninety thousand six hundred and seventy-two dollars and forty-two cents and unsold land was then valued at two million three hundred and ninety five thousand five hundred and seven dollars.

During the palmy days of the Credit Mobilier following the adjustment of the differences with the Durant faction, thousands of dollars were spent in advertising and placing the stock. Display advertisements were inserted in all the prominent newspapers and paid agents located in all the important cities. The result demonstrated the wisdom of the expenses, as not only were large quantities of its stock sold but the prices obtained for it were greatly advanced.

No sooner was the completion of the road assured than did antagonism and hostility appear. For instance in 1867 a government inspector appointed for the purpose of examining and accepting completed sections of the road, refused to do so, until he received "his fee" (?) which he put at twenty-five thousand dollars, he being in no way entitled to anything from the Company. By his refusal he tied up the issue of the Government bonds, seriously affecting the credit of the Company at a critical time.

In Washington the lobbyists were demanding blackmail with threats of organized hostility. Speculators in Well Street were a unit in bearing the stock and in attacking the credit of the Company.

The stock of the Credit Mobilier up to the assignment by Ames to the seven trustees, had not met with anything like a ready sale. For reasons of policy, some of this was assigned to members of Congress, Senators, and other public men. Some being paid for, others had it carried on their account. After the crisis had passed, the value of the stock rapidly appreciated and in the forthcoming political campaign the subornation of Congress in the interest of the Credit Mobilier by the use of this stock was made an issue and occasioned a great outcry. The accusation was thoroughly investigated by two committees during the next session and it was clearly proven to have been unfounded, so far as members of Congress having received the stock as bribes, it being demonstrated that the Company had no further favors to ask from Congress and that the members receiving it had paid the market value therefor. Notwithstanding, Oakes Ames was called to the bar of the House and severely censured for having sold it to them. The facts were, popular clamor demanded a scapegoat and Ames was selected. This, and the anxiety and strain of the load he had been carrying proved too much for him and he died May 8th, 1873. After his death the voice of calumny silenced, his work and character received the recognition it so well deserved.

The cost of material used in the construction of the road was enormous, thus the ties brought from the East ran as high as two dollars and fifty cents laid down in Omaha. The rails for the first four hundred and forty miles one hundred and thirty-five dollars per ton. This was before railroad connection was established between Council Bluffs and the East. After that the price got down to ninety-seven dollars and fifty cents per ton.

The pay of laborers ran from two dollars and twenty-five cents to three dollars and fifty cents per day. Train men two hundred dollars per month for conductors, one hundred and twenty-five dollars for brakemen, two hundred dollars to two hundred and fifty dollars for engineers, and one hundred and fifty dollars to one hundred and seventy-five dollars for firemen. Telegraph operators eighty dollars to a hundred dollars.

At times the Company (Credit Mobilier) was paying as high as five hundred thousand dollars per month interest. And in fact it was claimed by several of the directors that the paramount reason for the haste displayed in building the road was not so much the competition with the Central Pacific as it was to get rid of the enormous interest charges they were paying and which they would cut off upon the road being accepted by the Government and the consequent receipt of Government Bonds.

CHAPTER IV.
Commencement of the work.

Selection of Omaha as Eastern Terminus--Celebration Over Breaking Ground--Speech, George Francis Train--Commencement of Work--Conditions October, 1864--Routes Considered.

The first move towards the construction of the road was the selection of an eastern terminus which by the Charter was left to the President of the United States. This was fixed by President Lincoln on December 2nd, 1863, the official announcement being as follows: "I, Abraham Lincoln, President of the United States, do upon application of said Company (The Union Pacific Railroad) designate and establish such first above named point on the western boundary of the state of Iowa east of and opposite to the east line of Section Ten in Township fifteen, north of range thirteen, east of the sixth principal Meridian in the territory of Nebraska."

"Done at the city of Washington this 7th day
of March in the year of our Lord 1864.
                                Abraham Lincoln."

Immediately upon receipt of advice as to the President's action on December 2nd, 1863, the citizens of Omaha regardless of their connection with the road arranged to break ground for the Union Pacific Railroad and to properly celebrate the commencement of the work and especially the selection of their city as the eastern terminus, which was accordingly done. The spot selected for the initial point was near the Ferry Landing and not far above where the Union Pacific shops are now located. This particular spot with the first mile of track constructed, was long ago swept away by the Missouri River.

The ceremonies were commenced by asking the Divine Blessing on the enterprise in a prayer by the Rev. T. B. Lemon, Pastor of the First Methodist Church in Omaha. The Reverend Gentleman petitioned that the road make one the people of the East and West. That it would result in peopling the waste places of the West; that it might lend security to those on the frontier, and other similar requests, all of which have been fulfilled to a degree that is past being coincidental. The first earth was then removed by Governor Saunders of Nebraska Territory, Mayor Kennedy of Omaha, George Francis Train and others assisting. Congratulatory messages were received from different parts of the country. Speeches were made by A. J. Poppleton and others, the day being wound up by a banquet in the evening. The speech of the day was delivered by George Francis Train, then in his heyday, which is so characteristic of the man and of the ideas then prevalent relative to the road and the results of its construction as to warrant the following somewhat lengthy extracts:

"I have no telegrams to read, no sentiments to recite. The official business being over and as I happen to be lying around loose in this part of the country at this particular time, it gives me a chance to meet some of the live men of Nebraska at the inauguration of the grandest enterprise under God the world had ever witnessed.

"America is the stage, the world the audience of today, while one act of the drama represents the booming of cannon on the Rapidan, the Cumberland and the Rio Grande, sounding the death knell of rebellion, the next scene has the booming of cannon on both sides the Missouri to celebrate the grandest work of peace that ever engaged the energies of man. The great Pacific Railroad is commenced and if you know the men who have hold of the enterprise as well as I do, no doubt would arise as to its speedy completion.

"Four thousand years ago the Pyramids were started, but they simply represented the vanity of man. The Chinese wall was grand in conception, but built to break the tide of invasion. The Suez Canal was gigantic, but how limited all those things appear in comparison to this enterprise.

"Before the first century of our nation's birth we may see in the New York Depots, some strange Pacific Railroad notices such as,

'European passengers for Japan will please take the night
train. Passengers for China this way. African and Asiatic
freight must be distinctly marked For Pekin via San
Francisco.'

"Ere ten years go by I intend to let the European traveller get a new sensation
by standing on the ridge pole of the American Nation and sliding off into the sea.

"One day a dispatch will come in--we have tapped a mountain of copper, nineteen miles square, later on--we have just opened up another field of coal--or--we
have struck another iron mountain this morning--when Eureka--a telegram elec-
trifies the speculators in Wall Streets and gold drops below par--at ten this morning
we struck a pick into a mountain of solid gold.

"The Pacific Railroad is the nation, and the nation is the Pacific Railroad. Labor and capital shake hands today. The lion and the lamb sleep together. Here in
the West are the representatives of labor and in the East are those of capital. The
two united make the era of progress. Steam, Gas, and Electricity are the liberty,
fraternity, and equality of the people. The world is on the rampage. Events are
earthquakes now.

"Ten millions of emigrants will settle in this golden land in twenty years."

Early in 1864 work was begun on the first hundred miles. The actual work
being commenced within the corporate limits of Omaha in February. About one
hundred thousand dollars was spent in grading a due westerly route out of Omaha.
This was abandoned on account of it being so hilly, and a route south and thence
west was adopted. The ties for this section were cottonwood from the Missouri
River bottom lands, treated with a view of making them last. It was found that the
treatment was not effective and for the balance of the road, hard wood ties from
Michigan, Indiana, and even as far east as Pennsylvania were used, some of them
costing as much as two dollars and fifty cents laid down in Omaha.

At this time there was no railroad completed into Omaha from the East. The
Chicago and Northwestern being the first to reach there, and its first train ran into
Council Bluffs on Sunday, January 17th, 1867. Consequently all supplies, other than
those coming to them via the Missouri River, had to be wagoned from Des Moines,
Iowa, one hundred and thirty-three miles.

On the Missouri River the Company had in service six large steamboats carrying supplies and material for construction from Kansas City where there was railroad connection with the East by way of the Hannibal and St. Joseph Railroad and the Missouri Pacific Railroad.

Everything had to be brought in, the country being destitute of even stone and lumber, involving great expense and delays. While the level country enabled rapid progress to be made in grading, it was almost impossible to bring forward the requisite material to keep up with the graders and track-layers.

The contract for the first hundred miles had been let May, 1864, to Hubert M. Hoxie. By its terms he was to receive securities to the face value of $50,000 per mile. Sidings were to be not less than 6 per cent. of the main line. Station buildings, water-tanks and equipment was to be furnished by him to the value of five thousand dollars per mile. Hoxie before this had been in the employ of the Company in charge of the Ferry between Omaha and Council Bluffs. In March 1865, his contract was transferred to the Credit Mobilier Company, which as has been previously stated, was organized by the promoters and insiders of the Railroad Company to do the actual construction. Several experiences with individual contractors had demonstrated that they could not be relied upon, in fact that it required more in the way of capital-influence, and omnipresence than any individual could exert, consequently all original contracts for the construction and equipping of the line were handled by the Credit Mobilier who subcontracted it with firms and individuals, they by their close relations with the Company and financial interests as well as by their wide ramifications, being able to purchase materials and supplies to better advantage.

Everything was still held at war prices, iron, ties, lumber, provisions, etc., while currency and the Government bonds on which they were relying, were greatly depreciated in value. Labor was scarce and only to be had at extravagant figures.

In the report of one of the Government inspectors, made in 1864, when the grading had progressed some twenty miles out of Omaha, he stated: "There are now some two hundred men employed on the work and a like number of horses and oxen, together with two excavating machines that are doing the work of many men. It is confidently expected that this Section (the first forty miles) will be ready to be laid with rails by June 1st, next." This he regarded as very commendable but as compared with four years later, when there were nearly twelve thousand men engaged and track was going down from two to ten miles a day, it seems anything else but satisfactory.

A great amount of the preliminary work in the way of reconnoissance, surveying, and even locating was done under Governmental auspices previous to 1860, most of it by officers of the army. All of their reports and surveys were by action of Congress given to the Railroad Company, thus saving them greatly in time as well as in money. In addition to the Government surveys the Company investigated and did more or less surveying before deciding upon the route to be followed through the Rockies.

In the report of the Government directors for 1866 they refer to the following eight routes as having been investigated during the preceding year by the Company, viz.:

1st Via South Platte River and Hoosier Pass. 2nd Via Platte River and Tarryall Pass. 3rd Via North Fork of South Platte River. 4th Via Berthoud Pass. 5th Via Boulder Pass. 6th Via Cash le Poudre-Dale Creek and Antelope Pass. 7th Via Evans Pass. 8th Via Lodge Pole Creek, Cow Creek, and Evans Pass. 9th Via Lodge Pole Creek and Cheyenne Pass. 10th Via Lodge Pole Creek and South Pass.

The first seven of these routes included Denver en route. Something that the Company considered essential and which was very reluctantly abandoned.

CHAPTER V.
Progress Made.

Completion of Eleven Miles--Excursion--Officers--Labor Supply--Ex-Soldiers--Methods Employed--Progress Made--Headquarter Towns--Rough Times--Competition With Central Pacific for Territory--Stations--Buildings, Etc.

As we saw in our last chapter, ground was broken at Omaha, December 2nd, 1863. This, however, was more in the nature of a jollification on the part of the citizens of Omaha over the selection of their city as the eastern terminus of the line,--it being under the auspices of "the leading citizens," organized and enthused by the irrepressible George Francis Train.

Grading was commenced in July, 1864, and track-laying the spring of 1865. The start was not auspicious, the line was originally located directly west from Omaha, but after one hundred thousand dollars had been spent, it was abandoned on account of the hills and consequent heavy grades, and two new lines were surveyed, one to the north and then west and the other south nearly to Bellevue, Kan., and then west. This latter was called the "Ox-bow Route" and was finally selected by the Company, notwithstanding violent opposition on the part of the people of Omaha, who feared that the Company would cross the Missouri at Bellevue, thus leaving Omaha out.

September 25th, 1865, saw eleven miles finished, and in November an excursion was run from Omaha to the end of the track, fifteen miles. This was gotten up by Vice-President Durant, who took an engine and flat car, inviting about twenty gentlemen to go with him on the first inspection trip to Sailing's Grove. Among the excursionists was General Sherman who gloried in the undertaking and expressed regret that at his age he could hardly anticipate living until the completion of the work. The party was very enthusiastic, and as the narrator naively puts it "as the commissary was well supplied, the gentlemen enjoyed themselves."

For a number of reasons the work dragged. It took one year to complete the first forty miles. The lack of rail connections east of Omaha were, previous to January, 1867, when the Chicago and Northwestern Railroad reached Council Bluffs, a very serious occasion of expense and delay. The work was new, those in charge were not at that time experienced, funds were scarce, and the credit of the Company not yet established, and as a result the average rate of progress during the first twelve months was but a mile a week.

The work of construction was in charge of Vice-President and General Manager, Thomas C. Durant.--The location, General Granville M. Dodge, Chief Engineer, formerly General of the United States Army and who had up to this time been in charge of the department. The operation of the line, forwarding of material and supplies, actual construction, etc., was in charge of Samuel B. Reed, General Superintendent and Engineer in charge of Construction. The track laying was done under contract by "Casement Brothers" (General and Daniel) while Mr. H. M. Hoxie was ubiquitous with the title of General Western Agent. Colonel Silas Seymour of New York was Consulting Engineer and Mr. W. Snyder, Assistant Superintendent and General Freight and Ticket Agent.

Another of the reasons for the slow progress made up to 1865 was the scarcity of labor. The surrounding territory had no surplus workmen and the East had not as yet grasped the idea that the road was actually under construction. With the disbandment of the armies, both North and South after the war, this situation was changed for the better. Large numbers of the ex-soldiers drifted West and were glad to find steady work at remunerative wages with the construction forces.

The Secretary of the Interior in his annual report for 1866 stated that out of fifteen hundred laborers employed on the Pacific Railways, three hundred were negroes and performed their duties faithfully and well, and he recommended legislation looking to the employment of more of the surplus freedmen on the same work. Among the officials,--engineers and bosses,--there were many who were ex-officers in the army. Thus the Chief Engineer had been a General, the Consulting Engineer, a Colonel, the head of the track-laying force, a General. This can best be explained by quoting from a paper on trans-continental railroads read by General Dodge, before the Society of the Army of the Tennessee at Toledo, Ohio, September, 1888.

"The work was military in character and one is not surprised to find among the superintendents and others in charge, a liberal sprinkling of military titles. Surveying parties were always accompanied by a detachment of soldiers as a protection against Indians. The construction trains were amply supplied with rifles and other arms and it was boasted that a gang of track-layers could be transmuted into a battalion of infantry at any moment. Over half of the men had shouldered muskets in many a battle."

The same facts are brought out by the following extract from a newspaper of that day.

"The whole organization of the road is semi-military. The men who go ahead (surveyors and locators) are the advance guard, following them is the second line (the graders) cutting through the gorges, grading the road and building the bridges. Then comes the main body of the army, placing the ties, laying the track, spiking down the rails, perfecting the alignment, ballasting and dressing up and completing the road for immediate use. Along the line of the completed road are construction trains pushing 'to the front' with supplies. The advance limit of the rails is occupied by a train of long box-cars with bunks built within them, in which the men sleep at night and take their meals. Close behind this train come train loads of ties, rails, spikes, etc., which are thrown off to the side. A light car drawn by a single horse gallops up, is loaded with this material and then is off again to the front. Two men grasp the forward end of the rail and start ahead with it, the rest of the gang taking hold two by two, until it is clear of the car. At the word of command it is dropped into place, right side up, during which a similar operation has been going on with the rail for the other side,--thirty seconds to the rail for each gang, four rails to the minute. As soon as a car is unloaded, it is tipped over to permit another to pass it to the front and then it is righted again and hustled back for another load.

"Close behind the track-layers comes the gaugers, then the spikers and bolters. Three strokes to the spike, ten spikes to the rail, four hundred rails to the mile. Quick work you say,--but the fellows on the Union Pacific are tremendously in earnest."

Or as another writer has it, "We witnessed here the fabulous speed with which the line was built. Through the two or three hundred miles beyond were scattered ten to fifteen thousand men (?) in great gangs preparing the road-bed with plows, scrapers, shovels, picks, and carts, and among the rocks, with drills and powder were doing the grading as rapidly as men could stand and move with their tools. Long trains brought up to the end of the track, loads of ties and rails the former were transferred to teams and sent one or two miles ahead and put in place on the grade, then spikes and rails were reloaded on platform cars and pushed up to the last previously laid rail and with an automatic movement and celerity that was wonderful, practiced hands dropped the fresh rails one after another on the ties exactly in line. Hugh sledges sent the spikes home,--the car rolled on and the operation was repeated; while every few minutes the long heavy train behind sent out a puff of smoke from its locomotive and caught up with its load of material the advancing work. The only limit to the rapidity with which the track could thus be laid was the power of the road behind to bring forward material."

The above description applies to the later period of construction, when the forces had become thoroughly organized and the work systematized. The following table shows the rate of construction:

Ground broken at Omaha	December 2nd, 1863.
Work commenced at Omaha	Spring, 1864.
11 Miles completed to Gilmore	September 25th, 1865.
40 Miles completed to Valley	December 31st, 1865.
47 Miles completed to Fremont	January 24th, 1866.
50 Miles completed	March 13th, 1866.
100 Miles completed	June 2nd, 1866.
247 Miles completed to the 100th Meridian	October 5th, 1866.
305 Miles completed	December 31st, 1866.
414 Miles completed to Sidney, Wyo.	August, 1867.
516 Miles completed to Cheyenne, Wyo.	November 13th, 1867.
573 Miles completed to Laramie, Wyo.	May 9th, 1868.
745 Miles completed	December 31st, 1868.
1033 Miles completed to Ogden, Utah	March 8th, 1869.

1086 Miles completed:

To Promontory, Utah	April 28th, 1869.
Formal connection made	May 10, 1869.
Regular train service commenced	July 15th, 1869.
Completed according to Judicial decision	November 6th, 1869.

The progress made was daily wired East and published in the principal newspapers. Thus in the "Chicago Tribune" items such as "One and nine-tenth miles of track laid yesterday on the Union Pacific Railroad" appeared in every issue.

During the construction of the line, headquarters were established at different points at the front, which were used as a basis of operations for the construction of the section beyond. These places enjoyed a temporary boom, some of them like Jonah's Gourd to wither up and die away, others profiting by the start are today points of importance. The first of these was North Platte, Nebraska, its selection being caused by the delay incident to bridging the river. This was the terminus of the road during the fall of 1866 and up to June 1867. During this time it was the distributing point for all the country west. The mixture of railroad laborers, freighters, etc., all of them with more or less money, inaugurated a rough time and was the beginning of the wild scenes that attended the construction of the line. The town during the winter had a population of five thousand and over a thousand buildings. With the completion of the line to Sidney, Wyo., in June, 1867, the rough element left and established themselves at that point, leaving at North Platte about three hundred of the more sedentary law-abiding class who had determined on that point for their home. In moving to the front, houses were torn down, loaded on cars to be taken to the new site and there re-erected.

When it was known that Cheyenne was to be the terminus for the winter of 1867-1868, there was a grand hegira of roughs, gamblers, prostitutes from all along the line and from the East. The population jumped to six thousand. Dwellings sprang up like mushrooms. They were of every conceivable character. Some simply holes in the ground roofed over, known as "dug outs," others of canvas, while some few were of wood and stone. Town lots were sold at fabulous prices. The only pastimes were gambling and drinking. Shooting scrapes with "a man for breakfast" were an every day occurrence, and stealing so common as to occasion no comment. It is said of old Colonel Murrian, the then Mayor of Cheyenne, that he advanced the City's script eighteen cents on the dollar, by inflicting a fine of ten dollars on those who "made a gun play" i. e. shot at any one,--and that it was his custom to add a quarter to the fines he inflicted, making them ten dollars and twenty-five cents or twenty-five dollars and twenty-five cents, with the explanation that his was dry work and the extra quarter was to cover the stimulant his arduous duties required.

Such conditions brought about an uprising on the part of the more respectable element. Vigilance committees with "Judge Lynch" in command, took hold and from his Court there was neither appeal, nor stays. Witnesses were not held to be essential. The toughs were known and the judgments of the Court generally right. At least the defendants were not left in a condition to make complaint or appeal. The Vigilance Committee during the first year of its existence hung or shot twelve of the desperadoes, and were instrumental in sending as many more to the Penitentiary. The effect was to compel the tough element to either leave or abide by the laws and to put the decent element in control.

The next headquarters was Benton, Wyo. In two weeks (July 1868) a city of three thousand inhabitants sprang up as if by the touch of Aladdin's Lamp. It was laid out in regular squares, divided into five wards, had a Mayor and Board of Aldermen, a Daily Paper and volume of ordinances for the City Government. It was the end of the freight and passenger service and the beginning of the division under construction. Twice a day, long trains arrived from and departed for the East, while stages and wagon trains connected it with points in Idaho, Montana, and Utah. All the passengers and goods for the West, came here by rail and were re-shipped to their several destinations.

Twenty-three saloons paid license to the city, while dance halls and gambling dens were even more numerous. The great institution was the "Big Tent." This was a frame structure, one hundred feet long and forty feet wide, floored for dancing, to which and gambling it was entirely devoted. A visitor to the city thus described it: "One to two thousand men and a dozen or more women were encamped on the alkali plain in tents and shanties." Only a small proportion of them had aught to do with the road or any legitimate occupation. Restaurant and saloon keepers, gamblers, desperadoes of every grade, the vilest of men and women made up this "Hell on Wheels" as it was most aptly termed. Six months later, all that was left to mark the site was a few rock piles and half destroyed chimneys together with piles of old cans. The city after a tumultuous existence of only sixty days had "got up and pulled its freight" to the next headquarters.

Green River, Bryan, Bear River City, and Wasatch were the headquarters successively. The first, owing to the railroad having made it the end of a division and located shops there, has survived; the other three are but memories.

At Bear River City, the tough element who had been driven out of the different points East, congregated in large numbers, proposing to make a stand, it being supposed it would become a permanent town. The law abiding element numbered about a thousand, the toughs as many more. Three thugs were hung for murder, and in a reprisal the town was attacked on November 19th, 1868, by the tough element. They seized and burned the jail, then sacked and destroyed the plant of the "Frontier Index," a printing outfit that followed up the railroad, issuing a Daily Paper, and which had been particularly outspoken in its denunciation of the lawless element. They then proceeded to attack some of the stores, but were met by the townspeople and in the pitched battle that ensued, badly defeated. They made an undignified retreat, leaving fifteen of their number dead in the streets. From this time on the tough element fought shy of the city and with the extension of the road, its business left. Today there is not a thing to indicate that a town of four or five thousand had ever stood there.

The tough element started in to make Rawlins one of the "Hells" but the decent element had had enough and proceeded to clean up the town--showing they proposed to stand no foolishness.

The last of the railroad towns was Wasatch located at the eastern end of the longest tunnel (770 feet) on the road. In fact it was the delay occasioned by this work that gave rise to the town. When the line was put down a temporary track was built around the obstruction so as to permit the materials for the track beyond to reach the front. This place originally had a machine shop, round house and eating station all of which were removed to Evanston in 1870.

Upon the passage of the supplementary Charter in 1864 the restriction confining the Central Pacific to the State of California was withdrawn and they were authorized to build for one hundred and fifty miles east of the California boundary. This latter restriction was also withdrawn by Congress in 1866, leaving the meeting point to be determined by the rapidity of the construction of the respective lines, or as the Act of Congress put it, they could locate, construct, and continue their line until it should meet the Union Pacific continuous line. With the experience of three years behind them and the Land Grant, Government Bonds and prospective earnings, not to speak of the element of pride ahead, the two lines entered into a race the like of which had never been seen. The rivalry extended from the Presidents of the respective Companies down to the boy who carried water to the graders. Both forces, justly proud of their achievements, considered themselves a little better than the other. One form of the rivalry was as to which outfit could get the greatest amount of track down in one day. The Union Pacific's forces led off with six miles, soon after the Central went them a mile better. Then seven and a half miles were put down by the Union Pacific; the Central Pacific forces not to be outdone announced they could get down ten miles inside of one working day. Vice-President Durant offered to wager ten thousand dollars it could not be done, and the Central Pacific outfit resolved it should be done. Waiting until there were but fourteen miles for them to lay, they started in and laid ten miles and two hundred feet from seven A.M. to seven P.M., using four thousand men in the operation. And then the Union Pacific outfit was mad. They claimed if they had massed their forces, made special preparation, etc., they could do better than their competitors, but they could not prove it for there was no more track to lay.

The Central Pacific people ran their grade east of Ogden to Echo Canon, this when their completed line was only built to the vicinity of Wadsworth, Nev. The Union Pacific Railroad located their line to the California State line and had their graders at work as far west as Humboldt Wells, Nev., four hundred and sixty miles west of Ogden. This line west of Promontory was never built, however, and it is said that one million dollars was expended in this way. As it was the Central Pacific had their grade established some eighty miles east of Promontory Point, thirty miles east of Ogden, and this when the Union Pacific were laying their completed track within a mile of and parallel to their grade. The prize was so great that every nerve was strained on the part of both contestants as to who should push their track the further. The advantages were about equal. The Central Pacific were somewhat nearer their base of supplies, their laborers were the quiet, orderly, and easily managed Chinese and then they were in comparatively good financial shape. The Union

Pacific, though farther from their base of supplies, were in railroad communication with the points of manufacture, their men, while turbulent and hard to control, were enthusiastic and worth three to one of the opposing forces. They were well paid, well housed and well fed, and were handled by men who had as a rule, army experience back of them and who certainly were "bosses" in the best and fullest sense. During the winter of 1868-1869 the advantage was with the Central Pacific Company. Their line across the Sierras was fully protected by snow sheds and they only met with one week's suspension of business from snow troubles during the whole winter, while the Union Pacific were blocked between Cheyenne and Green River for four long months. The rate of construction grew rapidly. During 1864 there were about two hundred men employed on the grading and track-laying. While it took one year to complete the first forty miles, the second year, the year 1865, saw two hundred and sixty five miles done, over a mile a day working time, and this was exceeded from that on. There were about two thousand five hundred graders employed in 1867 in addition to four hundred and fifty track-layers and from this number up, until the completion of the road. Their forces numbered twelve thousand men and three thousand teams, while six hundred tons of material were placed daily during the spring of 1869 when the contest was at its height. The maximum track laid in one day, was seven and a half miles. As the line progressed round houses were put up at Omaha, North Platte, Cheyenne, Laramie, and Ogden, each having twenty stalls, and at Grand Island, Sidney, Rawlins, Bitter Creek, Medicine Bow and Bryan, of ten stalls each. These were substantial buildings of brick or stone with sheet-iron roofs thoroughly fire proof.

In addition to the large shops at Omaha where much of the building of equipment was done, repair shops were built at Cheyenne and Laramie.

Stations were established at an average of fourteen miles apart. The station buildings were built of wood and of two classes, three-fourths of them twenty-five by forty feet, the remaining one-fourth thirty-six by sixty feet. At each station water tanks were erected, surmounted by wind mills. Sidings three thousand feet long were located at each station and in some cases at points intermediate fifteen hundred feet long. In all there was about six per cent of the main line distance in side tracks.

To accommodate not only the Public, but their own employees, the Company put up good sized hotels at North Platte, Cheyenne, Laramie and Rawlins.

Eating houses were established at Grand Island, North Platte, Sidney, Cheyenne, Laramie, Rawlins, Bryan (Near Granger long ago passed out of existence) Wasatch (afterwards removed to Evanston) and Ogden. During construction days the charge for a meal was a dollar and a quarter, but with the opening of the road this was reduced to one dollar and afterwards to the present price seventy-five cents.

CHAPTER VI.
Indian Troubles during construction.

History of 1864-1865-1866-1867-1868 and 1869--Government Posts Established--Major North and His Pawnees--Ex-Soldiers Ogallala--Plum Creek--Sidney--Battle At Julesburg.

The country through which the Union Pacific Railroad was built was the hunting grounds of the Pawnee, Sioux, Arapahoes, Crows, Blackfeet, Bannock, Snake and Shoshones, the first three on the plains and the others to the west. These were among the most warlike tribes of the West, and during the construction of the road they were the occasion of serious trouble, not to speak of the annoyance and delay as well as the extra expense occasioned.

The following summarizes the conditions existing on the plains during the time the road was under construction.

During the summer of 1864, the whole line of the Overland Stage from St. Joseph, Mo., to Salt Lake City, was subject to Indian depredations, so much so, that Ben Holliday, its proprietor, asked the Government for five soldiers at each of the stage stations, and two to accompany each coach. Without these, he stated, he would discontinue the line.

The year 1865 was known as "The Bloody Year on the Plains," and its history is one constant account of attacks, skirmishes, depredations and murders by the Indians.

Notwithstanding the Peace Conference at Laramie in May, the year 1866, was not much better and the relations between the whites and the Indians were kept at a fighting point, culminating in the massacre by the Indians at Fort Phil Kearney of eighty-one regular soldiers.

The year 1867 opened with troubles all along the line. The Government inspectors reported "Indian depredations have caused serious embarrassment to the locating, construction and operation of the line. Constant and persistent attacks have occasioned great delay and expense." The Government aroused to the dangers of temporizing, pushed a large number of troops into the field, restored old and built many new posts. This, together with the ease of communication resulting from the rapidly extending railroad, had a deterrent effect on the Indians.

1868 was a repetition of the preceding year. A Peace Conference at Fort Laramie called for April was not attended by the Indians until November. Numerous attacks were made by them on the whites and the country kept in a turmoil. During the fall there was desperate fighting and the army assisted by citizens soldiers punished the Indians as they had never been punished before, resulting in a much better condition of affairs during 1869 and thereafter. Nearly all the Indian troubles occurred on the plains and east of Cheyenne. West thereof, either owing to better organization on the part of the railroad and military, or else to the intimidation of the tribes, there was but little annoyance from this source.

The surveying parties were as a rule accompanied by a small detachment of regulars and to this fact may be attributed their comparative small loss of life. While they lost but few of their number, still they were compelled to work at great disadvantage and frequently brought to a full stop by the presence of war parties in numbers too great to be ignored.

They, the surveying and engineering parties, were not so strong numerically as the grading outfits and did not have their resources. The different parties not only were frequently driven in but a number of them were obliged to fight for their lives. The station Hilldale, Wyo., perpetuates the name of one engineer, Mr. Hill, who was killed near this place by the Indians while locating the road. Another victim of the Indians was Colonel Percy in charge of an engineering party on the preliminary survey. He was surprised by a party of them twenty-four miles west of Medicine Bow, Wyo.--retreating to a cabin he stood them off for three days, at the end of which time they managed to set fire to the building and when the roof fell in he was compelled to get out, whereupon he was attacked and killed. This took place near Hanna Station, Wyo., which was originally called Percy in memory of the Colonel.

Realizing the necessity of military to protect the construction forces, the Government established numerous forts or posts along the line, viz:

Fort McPherson, Neb. (originally called Cantonment McKeon, then Cottonwood Springs Cantonment). Established February, 1866.

Fort Sedgwick, Colo., about four miles from the town of Julesburg, Colo.

Fort Mitchell, near Scotts Bluffs, Neb., a temporary proposition occupied only during the construction period.

Fort Morgan, Wyo., not far from Sidney, Wyo., established May, 1865, abandoned May, 1868.

Fort D. A. Russell, near Cheyenne, Wyo., established July, 1867, still occupied as an army post.

Fort Sanders, Wyo., near Laramie, established June, 1866.

Fort Fred Steele, fifteen miles east of Rawlins, established June, 1868.

Fort Halleck, twenty-two miles west of Medicine Bow, abandoned 1866.

General Sherman had prophesied that the influx of graders, teamsters, with their following would bring enough whiskey into the country to kill off all the Indians, and that the only good Indians were the dead ones.

One of the most valuable forces during the building of the road was a battalion of four companies of Pawnee Indians mustered into the United States' service under the command of Major Frank J. North, January 13th, 1865, this action being taken at the instance of General Custer. They proved most effective, notwithstanding their somewhat ludicrous appearance. They were furnished the regular soldiers' uniform which they were permitted to modify to suit their individual ideas and taste. As a rule their head dress was the customary Indian one of feathers. Their arms were the regulation carbine and revolver of the cavalry to which they added on their own accord, hatchet, knife, spear, etc., and when fighting was to be done they would strip down to the buff or rather the copper skin.

The construction forces at this time were being annoyed by the Cheyennes and Sioux, both of whom were the bitter foes of the Pawnees. Fort Kearney was the headquarters of Major North and his Pawnees and their duty was to protect the construction forces while at work.

As illustrating conditions existing, the following is of interest: A large body of Indians appeared on the scene near Julesburg, Major North and forty of his Pawnees started from Fort Kearney to the scene of the anticipated trouble. On the way he found the bodies of fourteen white men who had been killed by the Indians and their bodies mutilated beyond recognition, their scalps torn off, tongues cut out, legs and arms hacked off and their bodies full of arrows. On arriving at Julesburg, he found the place besieged. Falling on the Sioux, he put the whole band to fight, killing twenty-eight in the transaction. This party of Indians had but a few days before surprised a party of fourteen soldiers, killing them all. Soon after this trouble broke out with the Cheyennes. Major North and a party of twenty of his Pawnees started to look into the matter, and while out, struck a band of twelve Cheyennes. Taking after them, the Major was the only one who could get near them on account of his men's horses being tired out, but being better mounted, he was able to get within gun shot and killed one of the Cheyennes. Seeing his Pawnees were some distance in the rear, the whole party turned on Major North. He shot his horse, and using its body for a breastwork, fought the whole party, killing or wounding nine of them and held them at bay until his men were able to come up. This fight was considered one of the most daring on the Plains and added greatly to the fame of the Major and his Pawnees. After the completion of the road, Major North retired, and in company with W. F. Cody (Buffalo Bill) went into the cattle business near North Platte.

As has been stated, many of the officers and men engaged on the work were ex-soldiers accustomed to the use of arms. The construction trains and in fact all of the workers were liberally supplied with arms, principally rifles, and it was the boast that ten minutes any time was long enough to transform a gang of graders or track layers into a battalion of infantry. Every man on the work was armed, and it was the custom for the graders to carry their guns to and from their work, keeping them stacked within easy distance while at actual work.

"The front" was seldom bothered. As a rule there were too many at hand to make an attack attractive. It was the little detached parties or single individuals that were most often molested. After the rails were down, the trains passing to and from the front and the employees at the isolated stations and most especially the section gangs were in constant danger.

Among the first serious experiences was that of a construction train near Ogallala, Neb. A party of Sioux decided to capture it and compel it to stop; they massed their ponies on the track, with the result that there were some twenty or more dead horses, without damage of any consequence to the train. The trainmen used their guns and pistols to good advantage, resulting in a number of the Indians being killed. Later on, one of the Sioux of the party, on being interviewed, said, "Smoke wagon, big chief, ugh, no good."

At another time, the Indians succeeded in capturing a freight train near Plum Creek and held it and its crew in their possession.

General Dodge, the Chief Engineer, with a number of men, train crew, discharged men, etc., was running special, returning from the front to Omaha when the news reached them, and to quote the General's own words:

"They (the men on his special train) were all strangers to me. The excitement of the capture and the reports coming by telegraph brought all of them to the platform and when I called on them to fall in and go forward and retake the captured train, every man on the special went into line and by his position showed he had been a soldier. We ran down slowly until we came in sight of the train. I gave the order to deploy as skirmishers, and at the command they went forward as steadily and in as good order as we had seen the old soldiers climb the face of the Kennesaw under fire." The train was quickly recaptured.

Another incident occurred in the same locality, four miles west of Plum Creek, in July, 1867. A band of Southern Cheyennes, under Chief Turkey Leg, took up the rails and ties over a dry ravine. It so happened that the train was preceded by a hand car with three section men--encountering the break, the car and men fell into the ravine and one of their men was captured and scalped. In his agony, he grabbed his scalp and got away in the darkness as had his two more fortunate companions. The engineer discovered the break by the light of his headlight, but not in time to stop his train, and the engine and two car loads of brick, immediately following it, toppled into the ravine with the balance of the train, box cars loaded with miscellaneous freight, piled up and round about. The engineer and fireman were caught and killed in the wreck. The conductor, discovering the presence of the savages, ran back and flagged the second section following, which was backed up to Plum Creek Station. In the morning the inhabitants of Plum Creek, together with the train crews, sallied out to give battle with the Indians, but found they had departed. From the cars, they had thrown out boxes and bales, taking from them whatever had struck their fancy. Bolts of bright colored flannels and calicoes had been fastened to their ponies, which streamed in the wind, or dragged over the prairies. Major North and his Pawnees were at the front scattered in small detachments between Sidney and Laramie; within twenty-four hours they arrived on the scene in a special train. Following the trail, in about ten days they fell upon the Cheyennes, one hundred and fifty in number, and killed fifteen, taking two prisoners, one of them the nephew of Turkey Leg, their chief.

Another occurrence took place in April, 1868, near Elm Creek Station, a band of Sioux attacked, killed and scalped a section gang of five, and on the same day attacked the station of Sidney, coming out on the bluff above it and firing down on the town. At the time of the attack, two conductors were fishing in Lodge Pole Creek, a little way below the station; They were discovered by the Indians, who charged on them and shot one who fell forward as if killed. The other happened to have a pistol on his person with which he kept them at a distance until he reached the station, where he arrived with four arrows sticking in him and some four or five other bullet and arrow wounds, none of which proved serious. His companion also recovered.

Another serious attack was made on a train near Ogallala Station in September, 1868. The ends of two opposite rails were raised so as to penetrate the cylinders, the engine going over into the ditch and the cars piling up on top of it. The fireman was caught in the wreck and burned to death, the engineer and forward brakeman, riding on the engine, escaped unhurt. The train crew and passengers being armed, defended the train, keeping the Indians off until a wrecking train and crew arrived. Word being sent to Major North, who was at Willow Island, with one Company of his Pawnees, he came to the scene, followed the Indians and overtaking them, two were killed, the balance escaping. The following month the same party attacked a section gang near Potter Station, driving them in and running off a bunch of twenty horses and mules. About fifteen of Major North's Pawnees started in pursuit, overtook and killed two and recovered the greater part of the stolen stock.

The great battle of construction days occurred near Julesburg in July, 1869. The regulars, under General Carr, and the Pawnees (one hundred and fifty); under Major North, had put in two months scouting for several bands of Cheyennes and Sioux that had been raiding through the Republican and Solomon Valleys, attacking settlements, burning houses, killing and scalping men, women and children and raising Cain generally. They ran them to earth near Summit Springs where they were encamped. On July 11th, they surprised and attacked the Indians who were under the leadership of Tall Bull, a noted Cheyenne Chief. One hundred and sixty warriors were slain, among them Tall Bull. He was seen as the attack was made, mounted upon his horse with his squaw and child behind him trying to escape. Being headed off, he rode into a draw or pocket in the side of a ravine where some fifteen other warriors had taken refuge. He had been riding on a very fine horse, this he took to the mouth of the draw and shot. He then sent his squaw and child out to give themselves up; this they did, the squaw approaching Major North with hands raised in token of submission. She then advised the Major there were still seven warriors alive in the draw, entreating that their lives be spared. As the Indians were shooting at every man they caught sight of, it was impossible to save them and they were finally shot down. Among the prisoners taken was a white woman who had been captured by the Indians on one of their raids. She had been appropriated by Tall Bull as his squaw, and when the village had been attacked, he had shot her and left her in his tepee supposedly dead. Soon after the fight commenced, she was found by one of the officers who, entering in the lodge, saw her in a sitting position with blood running down her waist. She was a German, unable to speak English, and up to this time had supposed the fight was between Indians. On realizing that white men were in the vicinity and thinking when he started to leave her, that she was about to be deserted, she clasped him around his legs and in the most pitiful manner, begged him by signs and with tears not to leave her to the savages. After the fight she was taken to Fort Sedgwick where she recovered, and in a few months afterwards married a soldier whose time had expired. During the fight the troops captured nearly six hundred head of horses and mules, together with an immense amount of miscellaneous plunder, including nineteen hundred dollars in twenty dollar gold pieces that had been taken from the German woman's father at the time he had been killed and she captured. Of this sum, nine hundred dollars was turned over to the woman; six hundred dollars by the Pawnees, and the balance by the regulars. Had the latter been as generous as the scouts when the appeal for its restoration was made, every dollar would have been returned.

The above incidents are but a few out of thousands that occurred during the stormy construction days. They illustrate the trials and dangers encountered by the hardy pioneers. It was not only at "the front" that trouble was incurred, but after the building had proceeded, the section men, station employees and train crews were in constant danger. At the stations, it was a rule to build sod forts connected by underground passage with the living quarters to which retreat could be had in case of Indian attacks. For some time small squads of soldiers were stationed at every station and section house along the line, being quartered in sod barracks.

With the completion of the road and the establishment of regular train service, immigration soon poured in to such an extent as to make the settlers numerous enough to protect themselves, and it was not long until "Lo," like the buffalo, was only a memory.

CHAPTER VII.
The Builders.

Their Material and Methods--Oakes Ames (Financier)--George Francis Train (Promoter)--John A. Dix (First President)--Thomas C. Durant (Vice President and President)--Granville M. Dodge (Chief Engineer)--Subordinate Officials--Casement Brothers, Track-layers, Mormons--Materials Used--Their Source--Methods.

At Sherman Station, the highest point on the Union Pacific Railroad, stands a monument some sixty feet square and about the same height, bearing the simple legend, "In Memory of Oakes Ames and Oliver Ames." This was erected in compliance with a resolution passed at the meeting of the Company's stockholders held in Boston, March 10th, 1875, which read as follows, "Resolved that in memory of Oakes Ames and in recognition of his services in the construction of the Union Pacific Railroad to which he devoted his means and his best energies with a courage, fidelity, and integrity unsurpassed in the history of railroad construction, the directors (of this Company) are requested to take measure in co-operation with such friends as may desire to contribute, for the erection at some point in the line of the road, of a suitable and permanent monument." (By the recent shortening of the line this monument has been left some three miles away from the present track. Its removal to Cheyenne Depot Grounds or some other equally prominent position is under consideration.)

Oliver Ames was born at North Easton, Mass., January 10th, 1804; he passed his youth and early manhood assisting his father in the work of a farmer and later of manufacturing shovels, attending during the winter a country school. Serving first as apprentice, then foreman, he was in due time taken into partnership with his father to whose business he succeeded.

From twenty thousand dozen shovels turned out in 1845, their output increased to one hundred and twenty-five thousand dozens in 1870. A tireless worker dispensing with clerk or bookkeeper, his accounts were kept in his head. Over six feet in height, weighing over two hundred pounds, broad shouldered and massive in built. Elected to Congress in 1860 where he was kept until 1872. Becoming associated with the Union Pacific in 1865, at the time when the enterprise was languishing for lack of funds and it seemed almost hopeless. His attention was first directed in that channel by his duties as a member of the House Committee of Railroads in 1865. He was then a man of considerable means, recognized as an authority on business matters, and he enjoyed the confidence of President Lincoln and other prominent men of that day to a marked degree. In fact, it was at the urgent solicitation of the President that he undertook the almost hopeless task of financiering the construction of the road.

Entering into the undertaking with all of his energy and means, using his influence and persuasive powers with his fellow capitalists, he was able to raise by various means, the necessary funds for the construction of the line. Among others who took stock in the Company and Credit Mobilier were a number of public men, including Vice-President Colfax, Speaker James G. Blaine, James A. Garfield, afterwards President, and others of that ilk. The cry of corruption and bribery was raised in the campaign of 1872, resulting in investigation by Congressional Committees and a trial by the House, which rendered a very remarkable verdict, censuring Mr. Ames for having induced members of Congress to invest in the stock of a corporation in which he was interested and whose interests depended on legislation of Congress--but with the further finding on the part of the House Committee that no one had been wronged--that the Congressmen in question had paid him what the stock cost him and no more--that he had neither offered nor suggested a bribe--that their object in taking the stock originally was a profitable investment, and at the time no further action at the hands of Congress was desired.

Leaving Congress at the end of ten years' service, in 1872; he died from the effects of pneumonia during May, 1873, universally respected and esteemed, and the one man above all others who by financiering the proposition, was entitled to a monument at the hands of the stockholders of the Union Pacific Railroad. The following remarks made by him in regard to the road, at a time of apparently hopeless financial stringency, indicate quite clearly the character of the man and his views of the work:

"Go ahead; the work shall not stop if it takes the shovel shop. What makes me hold on is the faith of you soldiers," referring to the opinions held by the ex-soldiers employed on the construction. Or again, when it became evident that either the Ames' or the Railroad Company would have to go to the wall, "Save the credit of the road--I will fail."

George Francis Train may well be considered as the promoter of the Union Pacific Railroad. In season and out. Before Congressional Committees, public meetings, or to the unfortunate individual whom he succeeded in buttonholing "the Union Pacific Railroad," was the subject of endless oratory. In no small degree was he responsible for the opinion, "The road should and must be built," that became prevalent in 1860-1864, and which resulted in the action of Congress looking to the construction of the line. He was prominent in its affairs and largely instrumental in the formation of the Credit Mobilier.

As to the man himself, he was a genius, if, as a celebrated writer has said, "Genius is a form of insanity." A contemporaneous writer (George D. Prentice) thus describes him:

"A locomotive that has run off the track, turned upside down and its wheels making a thousand revolutions a minute. A kite in the air without a tail. A ship without a rudder. A clock without hands. A sermon that is all text; the incarnation of gab. Handsome, vivacious, versatile, muscular, neat, clean to the marrow. A judge of the effect of clothes, frugal in food and regular only in habits. With brains enough in his head for twenty men all pulling different ways. A man not bad--a practical joke in earnest."

Among his many undertakings were the Freeing of Ireland, Candidacy for the Presidency, Woman's Suffrage, Circumnavigation of the world. As illustrative of his character the following incident is apropos: While publishing a newspaper in England he was assessed a small fine, failing to pay which he was put in jail, where he preached to the prisoners on the rights of man and attacked the monarchy. The day following the authorities freed him on the ground that he was demoralizing the prisoners. Time has dealt lightly with him, and no one can read of his latter days--his brilliancy all eclipsed--a recluse except for his love and companionship for children--unmoved. In his day he was a power and in no small degree did he contribute to the living monument of great men--The Union Pacific Railroad.

The first President of the Company, Major General John A. Dix, was selected for the universal respect in which he was held. Secretary of the Treasury in 1861, resigning to go as general in the Union Army, he was the one man who it was felt would command confidence in the early days of the proposition, when the promoters had not as yet an opportunity to gain the respect of the financial world or of Congress. It was understood that he would not be able to devote his entire time or attention to the proposition, being in the Army at the time of his election. Still in no small degree did he contribute to its success. Appointed Minister to France in 1866, his absence from the United States made necessary his retirement. On his return in 1869, he was elected Governor of New York; and died greatly honored on April 21st, 1879.

The man who built the road was Thomas C. Durant. During the whole of its construction he was the man in control. He was Vice President and General Manager, with headquarters at Omaha; from the day ground was broken until the line was finished. He had been connected with several of the Iowa Lines previous to the commencement of work on the Union Pacific Railroad, mostly as contractor. As an organizer and director he was unsurpassed. In all the accounts of matters affecting the Union Pacific Railroad--hearings before Congress, Opening Ceremonies, Excursions given, appointment of officials and completion ceremonies, his name appears. He made enemies as do all strong men, and he also disagreed with his associates as to the best methods to pursue--still, he built the road, and after the man who persuaded the public it was necessary and the one who found the funds, he it is who is entitled to credit. Mr Durant severed his official connections with the road May 24, 1869, shortly after its completion, remaining, however, its largest stockholder.

The surveying and actual work of construction of the Union Pacific was done under the direction of General Granville M. Dodge. From 1854 to 1860 General Dodge was engaged in preliminary surveys for the Pacific Railroad, under governmental auspices. Entering the Union Army he reached the grade of Major General and at the close of the war entered the service of the Union Pacific Railroad Company as General Superintendent and Chief Engineer. To his ability and knowledge was due the location of the line and the rapidity with which the work was done. The General is still living--is in active service--having, during the last thirty years been connected with construction of many of the important railroads of the West, among them the Texas and Pacific Railway, Missouri, Kansas and Texas, International and Great Northern and Fort Worth and Denver City. He had been President of the Missouri, Kansas & Texas Railway; St. Louis, Des Moines and Northern Railway, Fort Worth and Denver City Railway, etc.

Peter A. Dey was the first engineer of the line, but left in 1864. He was not able to accept the methods of enormous expenditures the Company and the Credit Mobilier were adopting and retired on the ground that the Hoxie contract was made against his recommendation.

Colonel Silas Seymour was Consulting Engineer of the line during 1865-1866 and 1867, leaving it to enter the service of the Kansas Pacific Railway.

H. M. Hoxie was first in charge of Council-Bluffs-Omaha Ferry, then of the steamboats carrying construction material on the Missouri River, later Assistant General Superintendent, earning for himself the title of "The Ubiquitous." He died in 1866, while holding the position of Vice President and General Manager of the Missouri Pacific Railway.

S. B. Reed, Superintendent of Construction, was the man who had the handling of the forces at the front. He it was who ran the construction trains--fought the Indians and the toughs and bore the heat and burden of the day. He also made the surveys and located the line between Salt Lake Valley and Green River.

P. T. Brown, Assistant Engineer, was in charge of the advance survey under the direction of General Dodge and also located the line from the "foot of the Black Hills" to Julesburg.

James A. Evans was Division Engineer and in that capacity made many of the profiles, plats and estimates and final surveys. Also made the final surveys and location between Green River and the foot of the Black Hills.

D. B. Warren was Superintendent Utah Division; Colonel Hopper, Superintendent Laramie Division; L. H. Eicholtz, Engineer of Bridges and Buildings, and General Ledlie, Bridge Builder.

Among others to whom credit is due is Brigham Young, the then head (President) of the Mormon Church, and other prominent Mormons. The contract for grading from the head of Echo Canon to Ogden, known as "the hundred mile job," costing two and a half million dollars, was taken by President Young personally, and by him sublet in part to Bishop John Sharp and Joseph A. Young, the President's eldest son. They employed between five and six hundred men and the amount of their contract was about one million dollars. Other subcontractors were Apostle John Taylor, George Thatcher, Brigham Young, Jr., etc. President Young is said to have cleared about eight hundred thousand dollars out of this contract. East of his section the grading was done by Joseph F. Nounnan & Company, Gentile bankers of Salt Lake City, who sublet it to the Mormons. West of President Young's section the grading was done by Sharp & Young, the same parties mentioned above as sub-contractors under President Young. It was conceded that the Mormons carried out their contracts not only to the letter, but in the spirit. Doing some of the best work on the line.

The track laying proper was done by General J. S. (Jack) Casement and his brother, D. T. (Dan), with Captain Clayton as their Superintendent. They had in their employ as high as two thousand men at one time and worked under a contract that gave them a substantial bonus for all track laid in excess of two miles a day, as well as made them allowance for idle time occasioned by their being unable to work on account of the grade not being ready for them. Thus they were to receive eight hundred dollars per mile of track laid if two miles or less was laid in a day. If they laid over two miles in one day they were to receive twelve hundred dollars per mile, and for time they were idle waiting for the grade they were to receive three thousand dollars per day.

Many other names should be mentioned here and would did space permit, but will have to be omitted.

The men who built the Union Pacific Railroad are entitled to great credit and praise. They made money, much money out of the project, but they were entitled to it. Their success brought in its train the usual consequences, they have been accused of almost every crime in the calendar, assailed by the press, investigated by Congress, and sued by their less fortunate associates. Their achievement speaks for them louder than words and they can leave their reputations to history for vindication.

The line was originally laid with fifty pound iron from the mills of Pennsylvania for four hundred and forty miles and with fifty-six pound iron west of there.

As has been mentioned before, the first section was laid with cottonwood ties of local growth, treated by the burnettizing process, which was erroneously supposed would prevent decay. West of there hard wood ties from the East were used, some of them coming from far away Pennsylvania, and costing the Company two dollars and fifty cents laid down in Omaha. For the mountain section, ties of local growth were largely and satisfactorily used. The basis was twenty-four hundred ties to the mile on the plains, twenty-six hundred and forty through the mountains, and twenty-five hundred west of Laramie.

The lumber for bridges and building came from Minnesota and Wisconsin, excepting in the far West, where native lumber was used.

The grading was done to a very large extent by manual labor. It was before the day of the steam shovel or air drill. Pick and shovel and wheelbarrow reinforced by teams and scrapers were the means used, excepting where rock was encountered and then hand drills and black powder and occasionally nitro-glycerine were relied upon to quarry the rock which was very much in demand for masonry work.

The graders worked as much as two hundred miles ahead of the track. They were housed in tents, and all supplies for their sustenance and material used by them were necessarily hauled from the several terminal points. This resulted in the employment of a good sized army of teamsters and freighters. In the buffalo they had a food that, while cheap, was of the first order, and the number thus utilized was away up in the thousands.

No pretense was made to ballast the track, as the construction work was done. The ties were laid on the grade with just enough dirt on them to keep them in place. Speedy construction was considered of the first importance and then the ballasting could be done much cheaper after the track was down.

To a very great extent temporary trestles of timber were used, to be replaced later by more permanent culverts of stone. In some places where the piles were thus replaced by masonry, it was necessary to tear out the stone and put in piles again. The heavy freshets proved more than the culverts could carry off, and besides the stone work would wash out much quicker than did piles.

The bridges were mostly Howe wooden truss uncovered, with stone or wooden abuttments. Where the span was short, wooden trestles on piles were used.

One reason for deferring the masonry work as well as the ballasting was the inability to handle the necessary supplies. Every engine and all the equipment were kept in constant use hauling construction material to the front.

Notwithstanding what, to the contractor of today, would seem antiquated and expensive methods, the work progressed and made headway to an extent that has never since been equalled. It was the immense army, as high as twelve thousand men at times, that enabled this to be the case. One-fifth the number of men with modern methods and labor-saving devices would have been equally efficious.

The expense of hauling water and supplies for the army of men was enormous. The statement has been made that this cost more than it did to do the actual grading.

The great bugaboo of the day was the question of operating the line during the winter season, it being the general impression that the snow fall was so great through the Rocky Mountain region as to render it impossible to keep the line open. To ascertain the facts in regard to this as well as to obtain data as to the best method of overcoming the same, engineers were stationed at points where it was anticipated there would be trouble. For three winters they were kept in tents and dug outs to obtain information on this point, and on the spring and winter freshets which it was anticipated would be a source of great annoyance.

CHAPTER VIII.
Completion of the Line.

Connection Made Between Union and Central Pacific Railroads May 9th, 1869--Ceremonies at Promontory May 10th, 1869--Celebrations in New York, Philadelphia, Chicago, Omaha, Salt Lake City and San Francisco.

By the terms of the supplementary Charter of 1864, a great incentive was given the two Companies, the Union Pacific Railroad and the Central Pacific Railroad to get down as great a mileage as possible. In addition to the Government grant of Land and Bonds based on mileage, there was the traffic of the Mormon country and Salt Lake City at stake. Besides this, it was readily seen that the line having the greatest haul would be correspondingly benefitted when it came to subdividing earnings on trans-continental business. With these for incentive, both Companies put forth every effort to cover the ground. In the early part of 1869, rails of each Company were going down from six to ten miles a day. Records in track-laying were made then that have never been broken. Near Promontory a sign is still standing to announce "Ten miles of track laid in one day." Actual figures are not obtainable, but reliable contemporaries at that time stated there were twenty-five thousand men employed on the construction work of the two lines, as well as six thousand teams and two hundred construction trains. Both Companies were anxious to establish point of advantage that they could use in the controversy that was inevitable and which would determine the mileage and territory each was to enjoy. On April 29th, nine and a half miles remained unfinished. Three and a half for the Central Pacific Railroad, they having laid ten miles the day before, and six miles for the Union Pacific Railroad, the latter being the ascent of Promontory Hill and including a stiff bit of rock work. When the two tracks came together, the Central Pacific Railroad had nearly sixty miles of grading done parallel to the Union Pacific Railroad track--that is from Promontory east to the mouth of Weber Canon, while the Union Pacific Railroad had located their line to the California State line and most of the grading was done as far west as Humboldt Wells, Nev., four hundred and fifty miles from Ogden.

As stated the two tracks were brought together at Promontory on May 9th, 1869, but two rail lengths were kept open until the questions at issue were adjusted and also until a suitable program could be arranged for celebrating the event. Everything satisfactorily arranged, Monday, the 10th of May, 1869, was set for the ceremonies.

The Central Pacific Railroad completed their track up to Promontory May 1st. It was the intention to have the opening ceremonies on Saturday, May 8th, and the Central Pacific officials were on hand for that purpose. The Union Pacific party coming west were delayed some forty-eight hours at Piedmont by a gang of graders and track-layers, who not having received their wages side tracked the special train with Vice-President Durant and his party, holding them as hostages until the Company had paid over to the contractor some two hundred and fifty thousand dollars due him and which he in turn distributed among his men.

As early as 8:00 A.M. on the 10th, the spectators, mostly workmen of the respective companies, or other citizens of the railway camps commenced to arrive. At 8:45 a special over the Central Pacific Railroad came in with a large number of passengers. At 9:00 the Union Pacific Railroad contingent arrived in two trains and at 11:00 the Central Pacific Railroad's second train, carrying President Stanford and other officers of that Company, and their guests completing the party. In all there were about eleven hundred persons present, including a detachment of the 21st United States Infantry, and its band from Fort Douglass, Utah.

The Chinese laborers of the Central Pacific Railroad soon leveled the gap preparatory to putting down the ties and all but one rail length was finished. Then Engines Number 119 of the Union Pacific Railroad and No. 60 the "Jupiter" of the Central Pacific Railroad were brought up to either side of the gap. These engines were gaily decorated with flags and evergreens in honor of the occasion. A suitable prayer was offered by Rev. Dr. Todd, of Pittsfield, Mass. The remaining ties were then laid, the last one being of California Laurel finely polished and ornamented with a silver plate bearing the inscription "The last tie laid on the Pacific Railroad, May 10th, 1869", with the names of the directors of the Central Pacific Railroad and that of the donor. This tie was put in position by Superintendents Reed of the Union Pacific Railroad and Strawbridge of the Central Pacific Railroad, and was taken up after the ceremonies and has since that time been on exhibition in the Superintendent's office of the Southern Pacific Company at Sacramento, (Cal.) Depot.

For the closing act, California presented a spike of gold; Nevada one of silver; Arizona one of combined iron, gold and silver; and the Pacific Union Express Company, a silver maul. At twelve noon at a given signal, Governor Stanford on the South side of the rail and Vice-President Durant on the north, struck the spikes driving them home.

The two engines were then moved up until they touched and a bottle of wine poured over the last rail as a libation. The trains of the respective roads were then run over the connecting link and back to their own lines. Speeches and a banquet closed the occasion.

In the Crocker Art Gallery in Sacramento hangs a large oil painting of the meeting of the two engines. The artist having inserted actual portraits of many of the more prominent officials of the two lines who participated in the ceremonies.

By previous arrangement, the strokes on the final spikes were to be signaled over all the wires of the several telegraph companies through the United States, business being suspended for this purpose. First the message was sent over the wires "Almost ready. Hats off; prayer is being offered." Then "We have got done praying; the spike is about to be presented." Seven minutes later "All ready now; the spike will soon be driven." The signal will be three dots for the commencement of the blows. Connection being made between the hammers and the wires, the blows on the spikes were flashed over practically the whole telegraph system of the United States. At 2:47 P.M. Washington time, 12 M. Promontory local time, came the signal "Done" and the bells of Washington, New York, Chicago, San Francisco, and hundreds of other cities and towns announced that the American continent had been spanned, that through rail communication was established, never to be broken, that the Union Pacific Railroad was completed.

The formal announcement to President Grant and through the Press Associations to every inhabitant of the civilized world, was couched in the following language:

Promontory Summit, Utah, May 10th, 1869.

"The last rail is laid, the last spike driven. The Pacific Railroad is completed. The point of junction is ten hundred and eighty-six miles west of the Missouri River and six hundred and ninety miles east of Sacramento City."

> Leland Stanford, Central Pacific Railroad.
> T. C. Durant,
> Sidney Dillon,
> John Duff, Union Pacific Railroad.

No sooner were the ceremonies complete than there was a rush made to obtain souvenirs. In ignorance of the fact that the "Last Tie" had been taken up and an ordinary one substituted, the relic hunters carried off the substitute piecemeal. In fact some half dozen "last ties" were so taken in the first six months after the roads were completed.

An odd coincidence occurred at the closing ceremonies. The rail on the east was brought forward by the Union Pacific laborers--Europeans, that on the west by Chinese, both gangs having Americans as bosses. Consequently here were Europe, Asia, and America joining in the work, the Americans dominating.

Next morning the Union Pacific Railroad brought in from the East half a dozen passenger coaches for the Central Pacific Railroad, these being attached to the special train of Governor Stanford when he was returning to California, constituting the first through equipment.

All over the land the different cities vied with one another in celebrating the event--which it was truly felt marked the beginning of a new epoch in the history of the United States.

New York City celebrated with the "Te Deum" being sung in "Trinity," the chimes ringing out "Old Hundred" (Praise God from whom all blessings flow), and a salute of a hundred guns fired by order of the Mayor.

Philadelphia rang "Liberty Bell" and all fire alarm bells.

Chicago had a parade four miles long, the City being lavishly decorated, and Vice-President Colfax speaking in the evening.

Omaha had the biggest day in its history: a hundred guns when the news came. A procession embracing every able-bodied man in the town, in the afternoon. Speeches, pyrotechnics, and illuminations in the evening.

At Salt Lake the Mormons and Gentiles held a love feast in the Tabernacle and decided to build a few railroads for themselves.

San Francisco could not wait until the 10th. They started the evening of the 8th, when it was announced at the theaters the two roads had met, and it took two good solid days of celebrating to satisfy the people of that town.

It was rightly felt that the completion of the line was an event in the history of our country. It marked the progress of the West, united the Pacific Coast population with that of the East. It was the commencement of the end of the Indian troubles--assured the settlement of the West, and the development of its mines and other resources.

There has been but three general celebrations held in this country over works of public improvement viz: the Erie Canal, Atlantic Cable, and the Pacific Railroad. Of the three the latter was by far the more general.

The Poem by Bret Harte on this event is reproduced below:

What the Engines Said.

What was it the engines said,
Pilots touching head to head.
Facing on the single track,
Half a world behind each back.
This is what the engines said,
Unreported and unread.

With a prefatory screech,
In a florid Western speech,
Said the engine from the West,
"I am from Sierra's crest,

And if Altitudes' a test,
Why I reckon its confessed,
That I've done my level best."
"Said the engine from the East,
They who work best, talk the least,
Suppose you whistle down your brakes,
What you're done is no great shakes.
Pretty fair, but let our meeting,
Be a different kind of greeting,
Let these folks with champagne stuffing,
Not the engines do the puffing.

"Listen where Atlanta beats,
Shores of-snow and summer heats.
Where the Indian Autumn skies
Paint the woods with wampum dyes.
I have chased the flying sun,
Seeing all that he looked upon,
Blessing all that he blest.
Nursing in my iron-breast;
All his vivifying heat.
All his clouds about my crest
And before my flying feet
Every shadow must retreat."

Said the Western Engine, "phew!"
And a long whistle blew,
"Come now, really that's the oddest
Talk for one so modest.
You brag of your East, you do,
Why, I bring the East to you.
All the Orient, all Cathay
Find me through the shortest way

And the sun you follow here
Rises in my hemisphere.
Really if one must be rude,
Length, my friend, ain't longitude."

Said the Union, "don't reflect, or
I'll run over some director,"
Said the Central, "I'm Pacific
But when riled, I'm quite terrific,
Yet today we shall not quarrel
Just to show these folks this moral
How two engines In their vision
Once have met without collision."
That is what the engines said;
Unreported and unread,
Spoken slightly through the nose
With a whistle at the close.'

The first through train reached Omaha May 6th, arriving in two sections and bringing about five hundred passengers.

Although through trains were on regular schedule commencing with May 11th, it was not until November 6th, 1869, that the road was actually completed (according to Judicial decision.) Congress to make sure of the fact, authorized the President by resolution passed April 10th, 1869, to appoint a board of five "eminent" citizens to examine and report on the condition of the road and what would be required to bring it up to first class condition. This board duly reported in October, 1869, that the line was all right, but that a million and a half could be spent to advantage in ballasting, terminal facilities, depots, equipment, etc. On the strength of which the wise-acres decided the road could not be considered complete and withheld a million dollars worth of bonds due under the charter act. It was October 1st, 1874, before the fact that the line was actually completed sifted through departmental red tape, and the Secretary of Interior on the further report of "three eminent citizens" discovered that the road had been completed November 6th, 1869 as reported by the previous board of five, and further that the total cost of the line had been one hundred and fifteen million, two hundred and fourteen thousand, five hundred and eighty-seven dollars and seventy-nine cents, as shown by the books of the Company.

For a while business was interchanged at Promontory, but it was but a short time until the two Companies got together and an agreement was reached by which Ogden should be the terminus, and that the Central Pacific Railroad Company should purchase at cost price two million, six hundred and ninety-eight thousand, six hundred and twenty dollars the line from a point five miles west of Ogden to the connection at Promontory. This five miles was subsequently sold to the Central Pacific Railroad. This arrangement was as the West puts it "clinched" by a Resolution of Congress, making Ogden the terminus.

CHAPTER IX.
The Kansas Division (Kansas Pacific Railway.)

Conflicting Interest on Location--Leavenworth, Pawnee and Western Chartered By Kansas--Plans to Connect With the Union Pacific at the Hundredth Meridian--Supplementary Charter 1864--San Diego Or Denver--Construction Work--Indian Troubles--Receiverships--Consolidation With the Union Pacific.

At the time Congress passed the Pacific Railroad Bill in 1862 there were three conflicting interests contending as to the location. First that in favor of the Northern (now the Northern Pacific) Route, second the Central, and third that in favor of the Missouri-Kansas location. The Northern interest had not developed to a sufficient extent to cut much figure, only having the support of Minnesota, Wisconsin and Michigan. The Central Route was backed by Chicago and the railroad interests centering there. The Missouri-Kansas Route had the support of St. Louis and the territory tributary thereto. The last two were sufficiently persistent to have both of them recognized. Accordingly the Charter called for the one line commencing at the hundredth Meridian and running west with branches of feeders reaching that point, one from Omaha (Iowa Branch, Union Pacific Railroad), one from Sioux City (to be known as the Sioux City Branch, Union Pacific Railroad), one from St. Joseph or Atchison (to be built by the Hannibal and St. Joseph Railroad, later known as the Central Branch, Union Pacific Railway, Eastern Division and then the Kansas Pacific Railway); this latter in connection with the Pacific Railroad of Missouri from St. Louis to Kansas City to be the St. Louis line.

The Pacific Railroad Bill of 1862 read, "The Leavenworth, Pawnee, and Western Railroad Company of Kansas are hereby authorized to construct a railroad from the Missouri River at the mouth at the Kansas River where it should connect with the Pacific Railroad of Missouri (now the Missouri Pacific Railroad) to the hundredth Meridian of longitude upon the same terms and conditions as applied to the construction of the Pacific Railroad which it was to meet and connect with at the meridian point named." Through Kansas it was to be located so as to make connections with the several railroads through Iowa and Missouri, provided it could be done without deviating from the general direction of the whole line to the Pacific Coast. It further specified that two hundred miles should be built within the first two years and one hundred miles a year thereafter, and after finishing their own line they could unite on equal terms with the Union Pacific Railroad Company in the construction of the latter's line west of the hundredth-Meridian. This gave them the alternate sections of land within five miles on either side and United States Bonds to the amount of sixteen thousand dollars per mile,--similar to the aid extended the Union Pacific Railroad Company by the Government.

The Leavenworth, Pawnee and Western Railroad Company had been incorporated by the legislature of the state of Kansas in 1855, and was organized in January, 1857, but nothing was done of any consequence under its state Charter. The Company was re-organized June, 1863, and changed its name to harmonize with the Act of Congress to "Union Pacific Railway, Eastern Division." Under its state Charter it was to have extended from Leavenworth, Kan., on the East to Pawnee, Kan. (Fort Riley) on the West, with the privilege of building on west to the Kansas State line,--the state charter not permitting work outside of the Kansas boundaries.

Ground was broken on the line at Wyandotte, Kan., the state line between Kansas and Missouri, in August, 1863. Active grading commenced at Wyandotte, September 1st, 1863. The contract for the construction was first let by the Leavenworth, Pawnee, and Western Railroad Company to Ross, Steele and Company, but before they got down to actual work the Company had been re-organized as the Union Pacific Railway, Eastern Division, and had changed hands. The work was begun by Samuel Hallett who had been very prominent in promoting the latter Company, the contract being in the name of Hallett and Fremont. The Fremont being the erstwhile candidate for the Presidency of the United States. He is best known today as "The Pathfinder," from his several exploring expeditions between the Mississippi Valley and the Pacific Ocean. Fremont had been identified with the idea of a railroad to the Pacific in the interest of St. Louis, Mo. He, however, did not continue as one of the contractors but withdrew. It was a time of bitter feeling over the Slavery Question. Missouri was "Pro Slavery," Kansas "Free Soil." Hallett inaugurated his work by planting a post inscribed on the Missouri side "Slavery," and on the Kansas side "Freedom." Mr. Hallett was assassinated on the streets of Wyandotte, July 27th, 1864. An employee named Talbot had surreptitiously written the Secretary of the Interior in regard to the work not being up to requirements, more especially that the buildings were simply makeshifts put up to evade the law, etc. Through this and other complaints the Government refused to accept the first section of forty miles and withheld the bonds and land grants that Congress had granted. Hallett on his trips to Washington became aware of Talbot's action, and on his return called him to task with the result that Talbot shot him from a doorway as he was returning to his work from his midday lunch. After Hallett's death the work passed into the hands of St. Louis parties with John D. Perry as Director.

Under the Supplementary Pacific Railroad Bill of 1864, the conditions as far as the Union Pacific Railroad--Eastern Division as it was then called, were materially improved. It was authorized to connect with the Union Pacific Railroad at any point deemed desirable, but no more bonds or land grants were to be given than if connection were made as originally contemplated at the hundredth Meridian. It was also given the option of building from the mouth of the Kansas River to Leavenworth thence west, or of building directly west with a branch from Leavenworth connecting with the main line at Lawrence, but in the latter case no bonds or land grant would be given account the branch line mileage. Another feature of the Bill was permission to build on west to a connection with the Central Pacific Railroad, provided when it, the Union Pacific Railroad--Eastern Division reached the hundredth Meridian, the Union Pacific Railroad proper was not proceeding with the construction of its line in good faith. The Company under the discretion granted them elected to abandon the junction with the Union Pacific Railroad at the hundredth Meridian and to build directly West. The Company proceeded to explore the country South and West in search of a practicable route to the Pacific, which being found they then went further and had the several routes thoroughly surveyed. In their investigations they had four thousand four hundred and sixty-four miles chained and leveled. The most extensive survey on record.

Careful surveys demonstrated that the distance to the point of connection with the Union Pacific Railroad would have been three hundred and ninety-four miles from Kansas City, and this much of the line--Kansas City to Pond Creek, Kan.--was bonded-aided and land grant, the Government aid amounting to six million three hundred and two thousand dollars.

The Hannibal and St. Joseph Railroad reached St. Joseph, February, 1859, Kansas City, soon afterwards. The Missouri Pacific Railway reached Kansas City, October 1865. Owing to the fact that there were these railroad connections between the East and the eastern terminal of the line the work of construction was greatly facilitated and the expense of building the line greatly reduced.

The headway made was slow at first. The work was new to the officers in charge as well as to the men. The following table shows the progress made:

Sept. 1, 1863	commenced work at State Line (Wyandotte, Kan.)
Nov. 28, 1864	reached Lawrence--40 miles.
Oct. 30, 1865	first 40 miles accepted by the Government.
Dec. 15, 1865	50 miles done.
Aug. 18, 1866	reached Manhattan--118 miles.
Oct. 7, 1866	reached Pawnee (Fort Riley) 135 miles.
Jan. 7, 1867	to Mile Post 155.
April 8, 1867	to Mile Post 181.
Oct. 15, 1867	to Mile Post 335.
Fall 1867	to Mile Post 405 (Phil Sheridan.)
Mar. 24, 1870	reached Kit Carson--487 miles.
Aug. 15, 1870	completed into Denver.

The difference in altitude between Kansas City and the western boundary of Kansas is some twenty-seven hundred feet and is thus distributed--six hundred feet the first two hundred miles, seven hundred and sixty-nine feet in the next hundred miles, and thirteen hundred and twenty thence to the Kansas line.

The original intention had been to follow the Republican River, but this was changed and the "Smoky Hill Route" from Junction City, Kan., west adopted. When the road reached Monument, three hundred and eighty-six miles from Kansas City, dissensions arose among the stockholders. One faction was for building to San Diego on the Pacific Coast via New Mexico and Arizona, another was for building to Pueblo and up the Arkansas River, while the third and successful one was for pushing straight ahead to Denver and from there to a connection with the main line of the Union Pacific Railroad,--the idea being to secure for St. Louis a portion of the trans-continental business and the line the carrying thereof.

The line was built under contract by the following firms: Hallett and Fremont--Wyandotte to Lawrence, Kan., thirty-nine miles. Ira M. Schoemaker and Company--Lawrence to Mile Post one hundred and forty--a distance of one hundred miles. Schoemaker and Miller--Mile Post one hundred and forty to Mile Post four hundred and five--two hundred and sixty miles. West of Mile Post four hundred and five or "Phil Sheridan" as it was then called, the Denver extension was built by the Company itself, General W. J. Palmer being in charge.

During the construction of the line, the contract to feed the forces at the front was let to Goddard Brothers who utilized to a very great extent buffalo meat for this purpose. To procure these they employed W. F. Cody at five hundred dollars per month. During this engagement Cody claims to have killed four thousand two hundred and eighty buffaloes, earning for himself the appellation "Buffalo Bill" by which name he has ever since been known. The best heads were by special arrangement shipped to the headquarters of the Company at Kansas City, where they were nicely mounted and used as an advertisement of the road.

The line reached Ellsworth, Kan., the spring of 1867 and made for some time its terminus there. In all the history of "Boom Towns" or "railroad towns" there were none that surpassed this place. For ninety-three consecutive days there was one or more homicide in the town or its immediate vicinity--one hundred in all.

Another place that sprang into prominence during the time it was the end of the track was "Phil Sheridan" located near the point where the road crossed the hundredth Meridian, Mile Post four hundred and five. During its brief existence it was a rattling noisy place, full of life and vigor, rowdyism predominating. Not a stake, brick, or shingle is left to mark its site. It was here the construction rested for nearly a year and a half, financial troubles,--uncertainty as to whether to build to San Diego, Cal., or Denver, and some very fine work on the part of the Union

Pacific proper being the occasion of the suspension of work.

On June 26th, 1865, work was begun on the branch line from Leavenworth to Lawrence (Leavenworth and Lawrence Railroad), Major B. S. Hennings being in charge as Superintendent. Upon the completion of the branch in the spring following, the headquarters of the Union Pacific Railway--Eastern Division was moved to Lawrence, the operation of the line being under the direction of R. H. Shoemaker, Superintendent, who was succeeded in December, 1867, by George Noble. The work of construction was in charge of General W. W. Wright.

At the meeting of the Company held April 1st, 1867, Mr. John D. Perry of St. Louis was elected President, Mr. Adolph Meier of the same place Vice-President, and among the directors was Thomas A. Scott, of Philadelphia, (afterwards President of the Pennsylvania Railroad.)

In 1864 the population of the State of Kansas was one hundred and thirty-five thousand eight hundred and seven and in 1870 when the line was completed three hundred and sixty-four thousand three hundred and ninety-nine. This marvelous increase was due in no small degree to the construction of this line and the facilities it provided for the settlers to reach the cheap land in the interior of the state as well as the security it gave them against Indian depredations. Stage Lines between the Missouri River points and Denver had been running between St. Joseph, Atchison, and Omaha for several years, but after the line was built some distance the route was changed and connection was made between the end of the track and Denver by the Holliday Overland Mail.

Much trouble was caused by the Indians during the construction, even more than was encountered: on the Union Pacific Railroad. To this cause in no small degree were the delays of 1868 and 1869 attributable. It was necessary not only to arm the engineer corps, but also the graders, the Government issuing arms and ammunition for that purpose. Military escorts and guards were furnished by the Army to the Railroad men, both on the grade or ahead surveying. For the better protection of the road and construction forces Army Posts or Forts proper were maintained as follows:

Fort Riley	Mile Post 140
Fort Harker	Mile Post 230
Fort Hays	Mile Post 300
Fort Wallace	Mile Post 412

It was the Cheyennes, Arapahoes, Sioux, and the Utes who made the trouble.

In March 1869, the Company was authorized by special act of Congress to assume the name of the Kansas Pacific Railway Company instead of the Union Pacific Railroad (Eastern Division.) A witty epigram on this change that went the rounds of the papers at the time read as follows:

> The Union Pacific's about to apply
>   For a change In Its name and no wonder;
> Tis as warlike as Jove that great God of the skies,
>   And Pacific about as his thunder.
> And talking of this, it is strange as it goes
>   Through perpetual snows in some quarters,
> This railroad should be in the midst of its foes
>   Perpetually in hot water.

While those in authority had decided to push through to Denver, the idea of building through to San Diego was not abandoned, and in 1872 a branch line was commenced at Kit Carson destined to Pueblo and thence South along the Rampart Range to New Mexico and thence to the coast. This line was completed nearly due south to Fort Lyon and some twenty miles of grading done between Fort Lyon and Pueblo. Financial stringency together with the building of the Atchison, Topeka and Santa Fe into the same territory resulted in the abandonment of these plans and eventually the track from Kit Carson to Lyons was taken up under the following circumstances.

The owners of the Central Branch (Union Pacific), R. M. Pomeroy of Boston and associates, were pushing the construction of this line westwardly and announced their intention of building to Denver, thus making a competitor for the Kansas Pacific Railway. Mr. Jay Gould who at that time (1879) was the principal owner of the latter line, while out on an inspection trip over the line instructed his General Manager, "Sill Smith" Mr. Sylvester T. Smith to build into their territory and parallel them. Out of this grew the Junction City and Fort Kearney Railway (now a part of the Union Pacific Railroad). Smith was unable to buy sufficient rails to build and accordingly took up those on the branch of the Kansas Pacific Railway, Kit Carson to Lyons, i. e. the Arkansas Valley Railroad and re-laid them on the Junction City Line. Some of the Arkansas Valley Railway bonds were owned in Holland and a representative of the Dutch happened along on an investigating tour, but was unable to find any road. The matter soon got into Court and an effort was made to locate who was responsible for the tearing up of the Arkansas Valley Railway. Finally General Manager Smith was put on the stand and frankly acknowledged what he had done--and that he had no orders from President, Directors, or any one. The question was then asked who ordered you to build the Junction City and Fort Kearney Railway and the answer was Jay Gould; and who is he, for at that time he was not the well-known man he afterwards became. At this point Judge Dillon obtained permission to interrupt the proceedings with a query as in whose behalf all this investigating was being done. The holders of the bonds was the reply--then that must be myself, for said he, I have here in my hands all of the bonds in question. Mr. Gould had quietly bought in the bonds while the matter was in the Courts, bringing the inquiry to an end.

The line cost for its six hundred and seventy-three miles, Kansas City to Denver, and branch, Leavenworth to Lawrence, thirty-six million seven hundred and forty-seven thousand three hundred dollars, or about fifty-two thousand dollars per mile.

In 1873 the road was unable to meet its obligations and was placed in the hands of C. S. Greeley and Henry Villard, Receivers,--a majority of its stock passing into the hands of interests friendly to Mr. Jay Gould about 1877. Complaint was made that Villard and Greeley were not the proper men to act as receivers, that they were antagonistic to the owners of the bonds--lacking practical knowledge, etc. The matter finally reached the Supreme Court of the United States who in remanding it back to the District Court ordered their removal and the appointment of one man and he a practical railroad man as receiver in their stead. Under this order, in 1879, Sylvester T. Smith who had been connected with the road in various capacities, including that of General Manager, was appointed receiver.

In 1879 the Company was re-organized and in January 1880 consolidated with the Union Pacific Railroad under the name of the Union Pacific Railway Company, the holders of Kansas Pacific Railway stock being given share for share in the new consolidated Company.

The basis of the consolidation being

	Miles	Capital Stock	Funded Debt.
Union Pacific Railroad	1,042	$36,762,300.00	$78,508,350.65
Kansas Pacific Railway	675	10,000,000.00	30,567,282.78
Denver Pacific Railroad	106	4,000,000.00	581,000.00
	1,823	50,762,300.00	109,656,633.43

CHAPTER X.
The Denver-Cheyenne Line (Denver Pacific Railroad.)

Proposition for Pacific Railroad to Reach Denver--Cheyenne Route Select-
ed--Branch Line Proposed--Denver Pacific Incorporated and Built--Pro-
Rata Controversy--Operated By Kansas Pacific--Consolidation With the
Union Pacific.

In the original plan for the Union Pacific Railroad it was the intention that
the line would run through Denver and from there directly West across the
mountains to Salt Lake. When the line was finally located it passed through
Cheyenne, leaving Denver some one hundred miles to the South, the reasons
for this being the much shorter distance via Cheyenne as well as the decidedly
better gradients that were possible via South Pass Route as against the routes via
Denver and Berthoud or Evans Passes. The Denver Route was only given up after
repeated efforts had been made to find a satisfactory line that way.

The City of Denver had for some time past been encountering a streak of hard
luck--Failure of some of its most promising mines in 1861--Division of the Citizens
over the Civil War in 1862 and 1863--Fire and Flood followed by the Indian War on
the plains in 1864 cutting off communication with the East--then the grasshoppers
plague with the diversion of the Pacific Railway. Vice President Durant had made
the remark "it's too dead to bury," and this it was that spurred its citizens up.

In 1867 the Authorities of the Union Pacific Railroad offered to build a branch
from some point on their main line to Denver, provided the citizens of that place
would pay for the grading of the line and furnish right of way and grounds for terminal. The citizens of Denver were sore at being left to one side on the great overland
route and gave the proposition but a luke-warm reception. It is true, County Com-

missioners of Arapahoe County, in which Denver is located, ordered an election in August, 1867, to vote on the proposition of issuing two hundred thousand dollars in bonds in favor of such a branch line. The election resulted in an overwhelming majority in favor of it, eleven hundred and sixty for to one hundred and fifty-seven against. The County Commissioners in their negotiations with the Union Pacific people coupled with the proposition certain conditions as to the route which the branch line should follow, which not being satisfactory to the Railroad people, they refused to accept the bonds on the conditions required.

On November 13th, 1867, George Francis Train addressed a public meeting at Denver on the subject of a connection between Denver and the Union Pacific Railroad and as a result the Denver Pacific Railway and Telegraph Company was organized five days later. On the day following the organization the directors met and elected Bela M. Hughes President, D. H. Moffat, Treasurer, and F. M. Case, Chief Engineer,--one fourth of the necessary funds being subscribed. An arrangement was made with the Union Pacific Railroad Company by the terms of which that Company was to complete the road as soon as it was ready for the rails. In other words the road was to be located, graded, and tied by the Denver Pacific Company, and ironed and equipped by the Union Pacific Railroad Company.

In connection with the Denver Pacific proposition an application was made to Congress for a land grant to assist in the construction of the road, but before this was acted upon the Kansas Pacific Railroad Company had agreed to transfer the land grant which they had been given by Congress so far as it applied to their proposed line from Denver North, and the application of the Denver Pacific Railroad to Congress was consequently changed to one for bonds. This was granted in 1869 to the amount of twenty-four thousand dollars per mile, or two and a half million dollars in all.

The grading was commenced May 18th, 1868, and the same fall was completed to Cheyenne, one hundred and six miles. Owing to the delay of Congress in acting on the bond proposition as well as on account of the financial stringency the Union Pacific Railroad Company was then encountering, the latter was not able to carry out its contract in regard to the completion of the Denver Pacific Railroad, and the arrangement was accordingly cancelled. An arrangement was then entered into with the Kansas Pacific Railway by which the latter Company took a certain amount of stock in the Denver Pacific Railroad and proceeded with its construction, completing the line between Cheyenne and Denver on June 22nd, 1870.

There was great rejoicing over the event. The last spike,--one of solid silver contributed by the miners of Georgetown, Colo.,--was driven by Governor Evans of Colorado.

The first engine to enter Denver was the first engine that the Union Pacific Railroad owned. It had been the first to enter Cheyenne, also the first into Ogden.

In 1872 the road passed into the control of the Kansas Pacific Railway Company by purchase who operated it until the consolidation of both lines with the Union Pacific Railroad Company in 1880.

The Kansas Pacific Railway was completed into Denver in August 1870, and immediately embarked in the through trans-continental traffic from Kansas City and points east thereof, via Denver and the Denver Pacific Railroad. This was, of course, in competition with the Main Line of the Union Pacific Railroad who in accepting business at Cheyenne were losing the haul from Omaha to that point. The Kansas Pacific Railway and the Denver Pacific Railroad people were insistent and with no little degree of correctness that under the original Charter the Union Pacific Railroad was compelled to accept business from all connections,--but the terms thereof were not fixed and instead of accepting a division based on the mileage of the respective lines as insisted upon by the two lines named, the Union Pacific Railroad officials demanded a constructive mileage that would result in their line from Cheyenne to Ogden receiving six tenths of their local rates between those points when the business was competition with their long haul via Omaha. An agreement to work on this basis pending judicial decision was made between the two interests in September 1874. The question would not down, it was brought before Congress, Courts, and Arbitrators constituting a "Cause Celebre" the Pro-rata controversy.

Out of this grew the building of a rival line between Denver and Cheyenne wholly under the Union Pacific Railroad's control--locally known as the Colorado Central Railroad. This line was comprised of the Colorado Central Railroad, Denver to Golden, sixteen miles. It was commenced on New Year's Day 1868, being the first railroad in the state of Colorado. Its extension to Longmont, built in 1871, and the line Longmont to Cheyenne completed in 1877. This line was some one hundred and thirty miles against one hundred and six by the Denver Pacific Railroad, notwithstanding which it was used by the Union Pacific Railroad as its Denver connection until the adjustment of the differences between the different interests, which was brought about by an agreement made June 1st, 1878, by which the Kansas Pacific Railway and the Denver Pacific Railway were to be operated by the Union Pacific Company. This was followed by an absolute merger of the three roads, in January 1880 the new combination being known as the Union Pacific Railway Company.

CHAPTER XI.
History of the Line since its completion.

Government Indebtedness--Absorption Other Lines--Receivership--Train Robbers--Settlement With Government.

Upon the completion of the Union Pacific the rates for both freight and passengers were fixed at what now seems a very high figure. Thus passenger fares locally were ten cents per mile. Complaints arising, the matter was taken up in Congress and steps taken towards the appointment of a Board of Commissioners who should have authority to fix rates, both freight and passengers.

The whole question of earnings and expenses of the line was an unknown quantity and as soon as experience demonstrated what was reasonable and just, the Company voluntarily adjusted their schedules,--until today the rates over the line are about on a parity with those charged by eastern lines through much more thickly settled states.

In 1869 the agitation looking to a bridge across the Missouri River in place of the slow and often unreliable ferry culminated, and on March 11th of that year the structure was commenced. Three years were required for the work and the first train crossed on March 11th, 1872. By an agreement made with the city of Omaha that city was to be made the eastern terminus regardless of the bridge. This, however, was upset by the decision of the Supreme Court of the United States declaring the bridge an integral part of the line and that it commenced in Iowa not Nebraska.

In 1870 the question of repayment of the Government Loans made in the shape of Bonds arose,--more particularly that of the interests accruing thereon,-- the bonds themselves not falling due until 1895-1899. It was a question whether the lines were to pay this interest in cash or through services rendered in transporting men, materials, and mails for the Government. The matter soon got into the Courts and their decision as rendered by Justice Davis of the Supreme Court of the United States so fully and explicitly covers the ground as to warrant the somewhat lengthy extracts given below:

In his opinion, Judge Davis said, "This enterprise (the building of the Pacific Railroads) was viewed as a national undertaking for national purposes and the public mind was directed to the end rather than the particular means to be employed for the purpose. Although the road was a military necessity, there were other reasons active at the time in producing an opinion as to its necessity besides the protection of our exposed frontiers. There was a vast unpeopled territory between the Missouri River and Sacramento which was practically worthless without the facilities afforded by a railroad for the transportation of persons and property. With its construction the agricultural and mineral resources could be developed, settlements made, and the wealth and power of the United States essentially increased. And then there was also the pressing want in times of peace even of an improved and cheaper method for the transportation of the mails and supplies for the army and the Indians."

The policy of the country, to say nothing of the supposed want of power, stood in the way of the United States taking the work into its own hands. Even if this were not so, reasons of economy suggested it were better to enlist private capital and individual enterprise in the project. This Congress undertook to do, and the inducements held out were such as it was believed would procure the requisite capital and enterprise. But the purpose in presenting these inducements was to promote the construction and operation of a work deemed essential to the security of great public interests. Besides it is fair to infer that Congress supposed that the services to be rendered by the road to the Government would equal the interest to be paid. Congress well knew that the Government bound itself to pay interest every six months and the principal at the time the bond matured, resting satisfied with the entire property of the Company as security for the ultimate payment of the principal and interest.

This settled the interest question and the next one to arise was the question as to the payment of five per cent, of the net earnings towards the extinguishment of the Government indebtedness, as provided for in the act of 1862, viz., "And after said road is completed, until said bonds and interest are paid, at least five per centum of the net earnings shall be annually applied to the payment thereof." By act of Congress, June 22nd, 1874, the Secretary of the Treasury was directed to require this payment, failing which, to bring suit. The Supreme Court decided this in 1878 that the Company must pay this five per cent and defined net earnings as what was left out of the gross earnings after deducting all the expense of organization, operation, or for betterments paid out of earnings.

In 1878 the so called "Thurman Act" became law, by which a sinking fund was established looking to the extinguishing of the Company's indebtedness to the Government. This sinking fund was to be made up of one half the amount accruing on Government Transportation, the five per cent of net earnings, plus enough more of the earnings to make up in all twenty-five per cent of the total net earnings, but not to exceed eighty-five thousand dollars per annum,--this sinking fund to be invested by the Secretary of the Treasury in Government Bonds.

Up to 1879 the policy of the Company was to transfer all through freight at its eastern termini, none of its equipment being allowed to leave its own rails.

Soon after the absorption of the Kansas Pacific Railroad and through it the Denver Pacific Railroad, the Union Pacific entered upon a policy of extension by the absorption of other roads and building of branch lines.

Under this arrangement the Texas lines--Fort Worth, Texas, to Denver, Colo., eight hundred and one miles--were completed and added to the system. This line was built under the name of the Denver, Texas and Gulf (formerly Denver and New Orleans), the Fort Worth and Denver City and the Denver City and Fort Worth Railroads.

In 1880 the Railroad from Atchison west--originally the line that was to have connected with the Union Pacific Railroad at the hundredth Meridian, known as the Central Branch Union Pacific--became part of the system by purchase and was leased to the Missouri Pacific Railway Company who have since that time operated it.

Another line added to the system was the narrow (three foot) gauge line from Denver to Leadville and Gunnison. This line was commenced in 1873 under a Charter from the Colorado Legislature, reaching Buena Vista, February 22nd, 1880 and

Gunnison, the summer of 1881. It was absorbed by the Union Pacific on January 1st, 1881.

The Utah and Northern was commenced in 1871 by the citizens of Utah and reached Logan in 1873 and Franklin, Idaho, in 1874. The means for building this road was raised by the people of Northern Utah with great difficulty, much of it being donated in labor,--in grading, track work, right of way, etc. After an attempt to operate as a local line more or less successful, it was sold to the Union Pacific Railroad in February 1877 and by them extended to Silver Bow, Mont.--Huntington. Ore., with a branch connecting the main line of the Union Pacific at Granger, Wyo., with Pocatello, Idaho, on the old Utah and Northern.

On May 17th, 1869, one week after the ceremonies at Promontory, the Utah Central was commenced by the Mormons, Brigham Young being President of the Company. It was completed Ogden to Salt Lake City, January 10th, 1870. The work on the line was done very largely by the Mormons in exchange for stock, its equipment being turned over to them by the Union Pacific as part payment (to the Mormons) for work done on the grading of the line.

The Utah Southern--Salt Lake City to Frisco, Utah, was commenced in May. 1871, and completed in June 1880, and absorbed by the Utah Central in 1881.

In 1873 the line from Julesburg to Denver was located and most of the grading done in that year and the two following. Financial stringency together with complications arising over their relations with the Kansas Pacific Railway forced the abandonment of the project. After the consolidation in 1880 the line was re-commenced, practically new grades being necessary. It was completed in 1882, the work being done under the Colorado Central Railroad Charter.

All of the above lines were absorbed by the Union Pacific Railway and were a part of that system up to 1893 when the total mileage reached eight thousand one hundred and sixty-seven, made up of one thousand eight hundred and twenty-three miles Union Pacific and six thousand three hundred and forty-four miles, owned, leased and controlled. On the 13th of October, 1893, the United States Court at Omaha appointed S. H. H. Clark, Oliver W. Mink, and E. Ellery Anderson, Receivers, and in the following month Frederick R. Coudert and J. W. Doane were added to represent the interests of the United States, this receivership being forced on the Company by the very general business depression of 1893 and the consequent decrease in traffic and earnings. At the time of appointing receivers for the main line, the Texas Line and the Denver, Leadville and Gunnison (South Park) were segregated and placed under the control of separate receivers. The Oregon Short Line and the Oregon Railway and Navigation Company reverted to the hands of the original Companies, and have ever since been operated independently, although the controlling interest in both lines is owned by the Union Pacific Railway Company. In all, three thousand one hundred and thirteen miles of affiliated lines were segregated from the parent Company. In February, 1899, the "Julesburg Cut Off"--Julesburg to Denver--reverted to the Company, having been operated by the Receiver of the Union Pacific Denver and Gulf Railway in the interim.

Among other troubles which the line has encountered during its thirty-eight years existence has been that of train-robbers. These were a class of men the outgrowth of Western desperadoism, now happily passed into history. Without the fear of God, Man, or the Law, they would singly or in bands attack trains, rob the mail, express and sometimes the passengers.

Among the most noted cases of this kind were the Big Springs Robbery, occurring September 18th, 1877, when a gang of twelve masked men took possession of the station at that point, bound and gagged the employees, cutting the telegraph wires, and upon the arrival of the western train took possession of it, securing sixty-five thousand dollars from the express car, and thirteen thousand dollars and four gold watches from the passengers,--then mounting their horses they rode off. A reward of ten thousand dollars for their arrest immediately followed and three of the robbers were caught and hung. About one half of the money was recovered when they were captured. It is said the balance of the gang were apprehended and dealt with by a frontier Court, 'Judge Lynch' officiating, this however is tradition, its truth not being known.

Another robbery was that committed by Sam. Bass and associates who held up the west bound Pacific Express train securing from the express car some sixty thousand dollars in gold. This money was all recovered and most of the band either killed or arrested.

Another great event of this kind occurred in the hills of Wyoming, west of Cheyenne during 1898. The first section of the Overland West Bound carrying the mail and express was flagged and brought to a stop. A culvert behind it blown up with dynamite to prevent the second section interfering, and the express cars were then looted and the robbers rode off. Persistent pursuit lasting for years, however, brought them one by one to justice, one being killed near Kansas City while resisting arrest, another killed at Cripple Creek under similar circumstances.

In 1897 (January 1st) the present Company, Union Pacific Railroad Company, was organized under the laws of Utah as successor to the Union Pacific Railway Company.

During the construction days, Wells, Fargo and Company operated the Express service over the line. On completion the Company organized its own express "The Union Pacific Railroad Express" which continued to handle the express until re-organized as the Pacific Express Company.

Congress was appealed to in 1893 to pass a refunding bill, but failed to act.

Numerous unsuccessful attempts were made to reorganize the property, but this was impossible with the debt to the Government in an unsettled condition. Finally in 1899 an agreement (see foot note) as reached between the re-organization Committee and the Attorney General by which the line was to be foreclosed and the debt adjusted. This was accordingly done in 1899. The account standing:

Amount due Government.	From Union Pacific.	From Kansas Pacific.
Principal	$27,236,512.00	
Interest	31,211,691.75	

Total	$58,448,203.75	$12,891,900.19
Less Sinking Fund	18,194,618.26	6,303,000.00
	-------------	-------------
Balance due	$40,253,585.49	$6,588,900.19

and these amounts were accordingly turned over to the United States Government closing the account.[1]

---

[1]   The agreement In question was signed by Sidney Dillon, President of the Union Pacific Railroad Company; Robert B. Carr, President of the Kansas Pacific Railway Company; W. A. H. Loveland, President of the Colorado Central Railroad Company, and concurred with by Henry Villard and

CHAPTER XII.
The Central Pacific Railroad.

Suggested By Theo. D. Judah--Huntington, Crocker and Hopkins--Struggle for Congressional Aid--Progress Made.

The preceding chapters in tracing the history of the Union Pacific Railroad cover in a measure the preliminary events leading up to the building of the Central Pacific Railroad,--its connection from Ogden West.

In addition to this there is a wealth of incident connected with its history that will well repay the student. The following are a few and but a very few of its salient points.

For some years previous to the time when the final act was passed by Congress--which was to provide those of the western coast with speedy and safe communication with the homes of their youth--the question of a grand trunk road had been discussed by Californians as a public, and as private individuals. Many self-reliant men were sanguine of success, could the project be rightly brought before Congress. This feeling grew among the people of California, until a man who sought office at the hands of the people could not be elected were he not a "railroad man," provided

Carlos S. Greeley, Receivers of the Kansas Pacific Railway.

It provided that the three lines should be operated as one property, under the general direction of the Union Pacific Railroad Company. The gross earnings to be pooled and apportioned between them on certain specified agreed per cents, based on the earnings of the respective roads during the preceding year, the arrangement to be binding for fifty years and to be subject to the approval of the Court in whose hands the Kansas Pacific Railway then was.

that office was one wherein the holder could injure the prospects of the proposed road. Through the counties where the line was supposed to run, the question was strongly agitated, for those counties were expected to assist the undertaking, by voting their credit in various sums. So eager were the people of the interior of the State to have the enterprise commenced and completed, that they were willing to accede to any terms which would insure the success of the enterprise and relieve them from the oppression of a powerful water monopoly, which controlled a majority of the shipping both via the Panama Route and around Cape Horn.

The members of Congress from California knew that their election was in part owing to this feeling, and that much was expected of them by their constituents. They failed not when the time arrived, but to one--A. A. Sargent--more than all others, is California indebted for the great work which now binds her to her Eastern sisters.

But we are proceeding too fast, overlooking, but not forgetting, another name, none the less honored because the bearer lived not to behold the final completion of the work he initiated and so earnestly advocated. Theodore D. Judah now sleeps the sleep that knows no awaking, but still his presence can be seen and felt in every mile of the grand road which his genius brought into being. His name was a household word in the West, for thousands knew and appreciated the manly spirit and genial mind of the earnest, persistent and sanguine Engineer.

In the then little hamlet of Sacramento, dwelt C. P. Huntington, "Charley" Crocker, Mark Hopkins, and a few others--warm personal friends of Judah--who, often, in the long, winter evenings, gathered around the stove in Huntington and Hopkin's store room, and there discussed the merits and demerits of the Judah theory. These and some other gentlemen became convinced that the engineer was right--that the scheme was practicable. They subscribed fifty dollars a piece, and, in the summer, Judah and his assistants made a careful survey of the passes in the Sierras. This was in the summer of 1860, and in the fall the engineer party returned, toil-worn and travel-stained, but vastly encouraged and elated with the result of their summer's work. So favorable was the report that fifteen hundred dollars were immediately raised to be used the following summer in the same manner. The summer of 1861 found Judah and his party in the gulches and defiles of the Sierras, earnestly prosecuting their labors. The result but confirmed the previous report, with, if possible, more encouraging details regarding country, cost, etc. Judah then visited many of the principal capitalists of San Francisco to obtain subscriptions for the work, but failed to obtain a dollar. "But this road--what is it? Nothing that concerned them. It did not represent capital. A poor engineer wanted to make some money, and had started the idea for that purpose." These wise men shook their heads, and sneered at the undertaking. "What can they do," said they, "even with their Charter from the State? They have no money--they are poor men. It's only a sharp dodge on their part. They think the road will be undertaken in time, and then when that time arrives, they will stand a chance to sell their Charter and realize a few thousands--that's all. But they'll be dead before a railroad will be built across the continent." Such was the general tone of conversation among moneyed men regarding the road in its infancy, and it cannot be denied that the people of California owe nothing to the capitalists of their State--not even their thanks--for aid in the earliest days of the enterprise. The bone and sinew of the people--the mechanic and the merchant, the farmer, laborer and miner--did all that could be expected of them. But the capitalists held back--and for good reason. They feared that the railroad would give the death blow to the monopolies in which they were more or less interested. Sacramento alone deserves the credit of having originated and brought to a successful completion the Central Pacific Railroad. When the State had chartered the Company, when only funds were necessary to insure the completion of the work, only two subscriptions were obtained in San Francisco, and one of these came from a woman.

In 1862, Judah went to Washington with charts, maps, etc., of the road. Sargent was there, as enthusiastic in the support of the measure as Judah himself. He drew up the bill under which the road was built. James H. Campbell, of Pennsylvania, and Schuyler Colfax (than whose there is no more honored name in California,) were his most efficient supporters in the House. In the Senate, McDougal, of California, Wilson, of Massachusetts, and Morrill, of Maine, also stood manfully by the measure. And there was fought the great battle. There, enlightened ideas, assisted by young and vigorous intellects, met and conquered prejudice and moneyed opposition, and opened a new commercial era in the annals of the Union. But it was not accomplished without a long and wearying struggle, in which the bull-dog pertinacity and fierce grip of Sargent was manifested. Day after day, for weary weeks, in the Committee of the Whole, Sargent and Campbell stood up alternately, and answered objections as fast as made, in short, sharp, close and cutting speeches. And night after night, they held interviews with Eastern Senators and Representatives, while at their side, supplying them with information on all desired points, sat Theodore D. Judah, the engineer, earnest and hopeful to the last. Senators did not nor would not believe that the road could or would be built. Said Lovejoy, during one of the debates: "Do I understand the gentleman from California to say that he actually expects this road to be built?" "The gentleman from Illinois may understand me to predict that if this bill is passed, the road will be finished within ten years," responded Sargent. People can now judge between Lovejoy's and Sargent's ideas of the vigor of the West.

The end came, the bill was finally passed, and the news thereof caused the hearts of Californians to leap for joy. Ground was broken at Sacramento, and work was commenced immediately. Another battle was to be fought, a financial one. Before they could receive any aid from the Government, forty miles of road must be built and stocked, which would cost at least four million dollars, for that forty miles carried the road far up among the Sierras, through a great portion of their heavy work. Money was "tight"--in fact it always is when a man wants some--commanding two per cent. per month in California. The corporators put in their entire fortunes. The city of San Francisco issued bonds in assistance of the work; the State and several counties also rendered material aid, but all combined was but a trifle compared to what was required. C. P. Huntington, then Vice-President of the road, went to New York for aid, but among the capitalists there he met the same answer that had been given to Judah by the moneyed men of San Francisco. Finally, he met with Fisk and Hatch, dealers in government stocks. They feared not the result of the scheme. These energetic capitalists with the promptness of young and active minds--while older capitalists were questioning whether there was really a serious intention of building the road--pledged their faith to furnish the Company with what money they required and when they required it. The sum ranged from five million dollars to twenty million dollars per year; but they failed not, the money was always ready. The success of the enterprise was now assured. The bonds of the Company were put on the market, and advanced rapidly in price, and soon the Company had at their command all needful funds.

When the summit of the Sierras was reached, the road was pushed rapidly forward. But long ere this was gained, when the Company was toiling among the mountains, jeers and taunts of derision could be found in plenty in the columns of California newspapers. "The Dutch Flat Swindle," as the road was termed by some of these far sighted journalists--when the Company was laboring to overcome the heavy grade near that town--has passed into a byword in California, and now is suggestive of success. The route, after the "summit" was gained, was then comparatively easy, and rapid progress was made. The Chinese laborers, who had worked on the road from first to last, drove the work forward, and on May 10th, 1869, the roads met on Promontory Point, six hundred and ninety miles from Sacramento. The following will show the number of miles completed during each year: In 1863-1864-1865, twenty miles each year; in 1866, thirty miles; in 1867, forty-six miles; in 1868 three hundred and sixty-three miles; in 1869, one hundred and ninety-one miles.

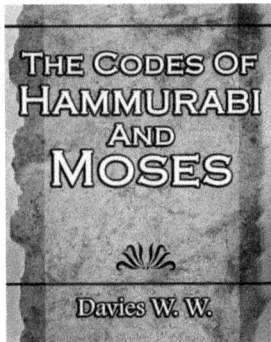

The Codes Of Hammurabi And Moses
W. W. Davies

QTY

The discovery of the Hammurabi Code is one of the greatest achievements of archaeology, and is of paramount interest, not only to the student of the Bible, but also to all those interested in ancient history...

Religion   **ISBN:** *1-59462-338-4*   **Pages:132**
MSRP $12.95

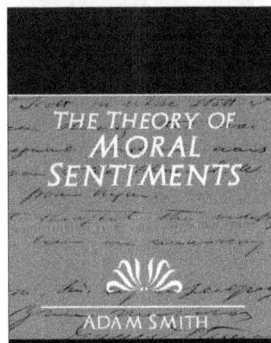

The Theory of Moral Sentiments
Adam Smith

QTY

This work from 1749. contains original theories of conscience amd moral judgment and it is the foundation for systemof morals.

Philosophy **ISBN:** *1-59462-777-0*   **Pages:536**
MSRP $19.95

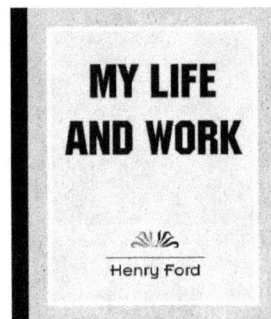

Jessica's First Prayer
Hesba Stretton

QTY

In a screened and secluded corner of one of the many railway-bridges which span the streets of London there could be seen a few years ago, from five o'clock every morning until half past eight, a tidily set-out coffee-stall, consisting of a trestle and board, upon which stood two large tin cans, with a small fire of charcoal burning under each so as to keep the coffee boiling during the early hours of the morning when the work-people were thronging into the city on their way to their daily toil...

Pages:84

Childrens   **ISBN:** *1-59462-373-2*   *MSRP $9.95*

My Life and Work
Henry Ford

QTY

Henry Ford revolutionized the world with his implementation of mass production for the Model T automobile. Gain valuable business insight into his life and work with his own auto-biography... "We have only started on our development of our country we have not as yet, with all our talk of wonderful progress, done more than scratch the surface. The progress has been wonderful enough but..."

Pages:300

Biographies/   **ISBN:** *1-59462-198-5*   *MSRP $21.95*

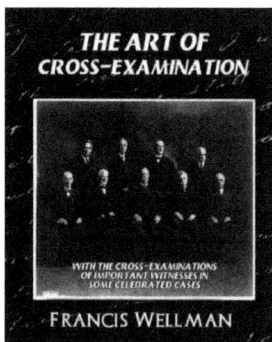

The Art of Cross-Examination
Francis Wellman

QTY

I presume it is the experience of every author, after his first book is published upon an important subject, to be almost overwhelmed with a wealth of ideas and illustrations which could readily have been included in his book, and which to his own mind, at least, seem to make a second edition inevitable. Such certainly was the case with me; and when the first edition had reached its sixth impression in five months, I rejoiced to learn that it seemed to my publishers that the book had met with a sufficiently favorable reception to justify a second and considerably enlarged edition. ..

Pages:412

Reference   ISBN: *1-59462-647-2*   *MSRP $19.95*

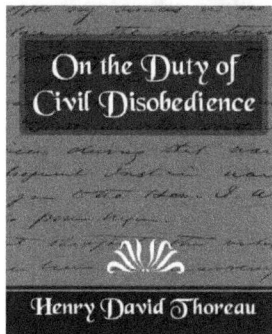

On the Duty of Civil Disobedience
Henry David Thoreau

QTY

Thoreau wrote his famous essay, On the Duty of Civil Disobedience, as a protest against an unjust but popular war and the immoral but popular institution of slave-owning. He did more than write—he declined to pay his taxes, and was hauled off to gaol in consequence. Who can say how much this refusal of his hastened the end of the war and of slavery ?

Law   ISBN: *1-59462-747-9*   **Pages:48**   *MSRP $7.45*

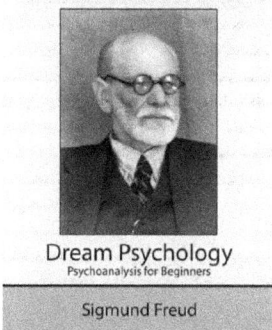

Dream Psychology Psychoanalysis for Beginners
Sigmund Freud

QTY

Sigmund Freud, born Sigismund Schlomo Freud (May 6, 1856 - September 23, 1939), was a Jewish-Austrian neurologist and psychiatrist who co-founded the psychoanalytic school of psychology. Freud is best known for his theories of the unconscious mind, especially involving the mechanism of repression; his redefinition of sexual desire as mobile and directed towards a wide variety of objects; and his therapeutic techniques, especially his understanding of transference in the therapeutic relationship and the presumed value of dreams as sources of insight into unconscious desires.

Pages:196

Psychology   ISBN: *1-59462-905-6*   *MSRP $15.45*

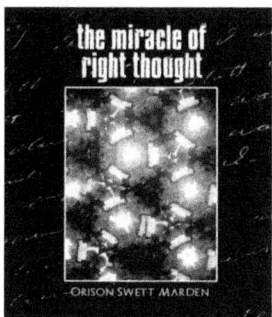

The Miracle of Right Thought
Orison Swett Marden

QTY

Believe with all of your heart that you will do what you were made to do. When the mind has once formed the habit of holding cheerful, happy, prosperous pictures, it will not be easy to form the opposite habit. It does not matter how improbable or how far away this realization may see, or how dark the prospects may be, if we visualize them as best we can, as vividly as possible, hold tenaciously to them and vigorously struggle to attain them, they will gradually become actualized, realized in the life. But a desire, a longing without endeavor, a yearning abandoned or held indifferently will vanish without realization.

Pages:360

Self Help   ISBN: *1-59462-644-8*   *MSRP $25.45*

The Rosicrucian Cosmo-Conception Mystic Christianity *by Max Heindel*   ISBN: *1-59462-188-8*   **$38.95**
The Rosicrucian Cosmo-conception is not dogmatic, neither does it appeal to any other authority than the reason of the student. It is: not controversial, but is: sent forth in the, hope that it may help to clear... New Age/Religion Pages 646

Abandonment To Divine Providence *by Jean-Pierre de Caussade*   ISBN: *1-59462-228-0*   **$25.95**
"The Rev. Jean Pierre de Caussade was one of the most remarkable spiritual writers of the Society of Jesus in France in the 18th Century. His death took place at Toulouse in 1751. His works have gone through many editions and have been republished... Inspirational/Religion Pages 400

Mental Chemistry *by Charles Haanel*   ISBN: *1-59462-192-6*   **$23.95**
Mental Chemistry allows the change of material conditions by combining and appropriately utilizing the power of the mind. Much like applied chemistry creates something new and unique out of careful combinations of chemicals the mastery of mental chemistry... New Age Pages 354

The Letters of Robert Browning and Elizabeth Barret Barrett 1845-1846 vol II   ISBN: *1-59462-193-4*   **$35.95**
by Robert Browning and Elizabeth Barrett Biographies Pages 596

Gleanings In Genesis (volume I) *by Arthur W. Pink*   ISBN: *1-59462-130-6*   **$27.45**
Appropriately has Genesis been termed "the seed plot of the Bible" for in it we have, in germ form, almost all of the great doctrines which are afterwards fully developed in the books of Scripture which follow... Religion/Inspirational Pages 420

The Master Key *by L. W. de Laurence*   ISBN: *1-59462-001-6*   **$30.95**
In no branch of human knowledge has there been a more lively increase of the spirit of research during the past few years than in the study of Psychology, Concentration and Mental Discipline. The requests for authentic lessons in Thought Control, Mental Discipline and... New Age/Business Pages 422

The Lesser Key Of Solomon Goetia *by L. W. de Laurence*   ISBN: *1-59462-092-X*   **$9.95**
This translation of the first book of the "Lernegton" which is now for the first time made accessible to students of Talismanic Magic was done, after careful collation and edition, from numerous Ancient Manuscripts in Hebrew, Latin, and French... New Age/Occult Pages 92

Rubaiyat Of Omar Khayyam *by Edward Fitzgerald*   ISBN: *1-59462-332-5*   **$13.95**
Edward Fitzgerald, whom the world has already learned, in spite of his own efforts to remain within the shadow of anonymity, to look upon as one of the rarest poets of the century, was born at Bredfield, in Suffolk, on the 31st of March, 1809. He was the third son of John Purcell... Music Pages 172

Ancient Law *by Henry Maine*   ISBN: *1-59462-128-4*   **$29.95**
The chief object of the following pages is to indicate some of the earliest ideas of mankind, as they are reflected in Ancient Law, and to point out the relation of those ideas to modern thought. Religion/History Pages 452

Far-Away Stories *by William J. Locke*   ISBN: *1-59462-129-2*   **$19.45**
"Good wine needs no bush, but a collection of mixed vintages does. And this book is just such a collection. Some of the stories I do not want to remain buried for ever in the museum files of dead magazine-numbers an author's not unpardonable vanity..." Fiction Pages 272

Life of David Crockett *by David Crockett*   ISBN: *1-59462-250-7*   **$27.45**
"Colonel David Crockett was one of the most remarkable men of the times in which he lived. Born in humble life, but gifted with a strong will, an indomitable courage, and unremitting perseverance... Biographies/New Age Pages 424

Lip-Reading *by Edward Nitchie*   ISBN: *1-59462-206-X*   **$25.95**
Edward B. Nitchie, founder of the New York School for the Hard of Hearing, now the Nitchie School of Lip-Reading, Inc, wrote "LIP-READING Principles and Practice". The development and perfecting of this meritorious work on lip-reading was an undertaking... How-to Pages 400

A Handbook of Suggestive Therapeutics, Applied Hypnotism, Psychic Science   ISBN: *1-59462-214-0*   **$24.95**
by Henry Munro Health/New Age/Health/Self-help Pages 376

A Doll's House: and Two Other Plays *by Henrik Ibsen*   ISBN: *1-59462-112-8*   **$19.95**
Henrik Ibsen created this classic when in revolutionary 1848 Rome. Introducing some striking concepts in playwriting for the realist genre, this play has been studied the world over. Fiction/Classics/Plays 308

The Light of Asia *by sir Edwin Arnold*   ISBN: *1-59462-204-3*   **$13.95**
In this poetic masterpiece, Edwin Arnold describes the life and teachings of Buddha. The man who was to become known as Buddha to the world was born as Prince Gautama of India but he rejected the worldly riches and abandoned the reigns of power when... Religion/History/Biographies Pages 170

The Complete Works of Guy de Maupassant *by Guy de Maupassant*   ISBN: *1-59462-157-8*   **$16.95**
"For days and days, nights and nights, I had dreamed of that first kiss which was to consecrate our engagement, and I knew not on what spot I should put my lips..." Fiction/Classics Pages 240

The Art of Cross-Examination *by Francis L. Wellman*   ISBN: *1-59462-309-0*   **$26.95**
Written by a renowned trial lawyer, Wellman imparts his experience and uses case studies to explain how to use psychology to extract desired information through questioning. How-to/Science/Reference Pages 408

Answered or Unanswered? *by Louisa Vaughan*   ISBN: *1-59462-248-5*   **$10.95**
Miracles of Faith in China Religion Pages 112

The Edinburgh Lectures on Mental Science (1909) *by Thomas*   ISBN: *1-59462-008-3*   **$11.95**
This book contains the substance of a course of lectures recently given by the writer in the Queen Street Hall, Edinburgh. Its purpose is to indicate the Natural Principles governing the relation between Mental Action and Material Conditions... New Age/Psychology Pages 148

Ayesha *by H. Rider Haggard*   ISBN: *1-59462-301-5*   **$24.95**
Verily and indeed it is the unexpected that happens! Probably if there was one person upon the earth from whom the Editor of this, and of a certain previous history, did not expect to hear again... Classics Pages 380

Ayala's Angel *by Anthony Trollope*   ISBN: *1-59462-352-X*   **$29.95**
The two girls were both pretty, but Lucy who was twenty-one who supposed to be simple and comparatively unattractive, whereas Ayala was credited, as her Bombwhat romantic name might show, with poetic charm and a taste for romance. Ayala when her father died was nineteen... Fiction Pages 484

The American Commonwealth *by James Bryce*   ISBN: *1-59462-286-8*   **$34.45**
An interpretation of American democratic political theory. It examines political mechanics and society from the perspective of Scotsman James Bryce Politics Pages 572

Stories of the Pilgrims *by Margaret P. Pumphrey*   ISBN: *1-59462-116-0*   **$17.95**
This book explores pilgrims religious oppression in England as well as their escape to Holland and eventual crossing to America on the Mayflower, and their early days in New England... History Pages 268

QTY

The Fasting Cure *by Sinclair Upton*   **ISBN:** *1-59462-222-1*   **$13.95**
In the Cosmopolitan Magazine for May, 1910, and in the Contemporary Review (London) for April, 1910, I published an article dealing with my experiences in fasting. I have written a great many magazine articles, but never one which attracted so much attention... New Age/Self Help/Health Pages 164

Hebrew Astrology *by Sepharial*   **ISBN:** *1-59462-308-2*   **$13.45**
In these days of advanced thinking it is a matter of common observation that we have left many of the old landmarks behind and that we are now pressing forward to greater heights and to a wider horizon than that which represented the mind-content of our progenitors... Astrology Pages 144

Thought Vibration or The Law of Attraction in the Thought World   **ISBN:** *1-59462-127-6*   **$12.95**
by William Walker Atkinson   *Psychology/Religion Pages 144*

Optimism *by Helen Keller*   **ISBN:** *1-59462-108-X*   **$15.95**
Helen Keller was blind, deaf, and mute since 19 months old, yet famously learned how to overcome these handicaps, communicate with the world, and spread her lectures promoting optimism. An inspiring read for everyone... Biographies/Inspirational Pages 84

Sara Crewe *by Frances Burnett*   **ISBN:** *1-59462-360-0*   **$9.45**
In the first place, Miss Minchin lived in London. Her home was a large, dull, tall one, in a large, dull square, where all the houses were alike, and all the sparrows were alike, and where all the door-knockers made the same heavy sound... Childrens/Classic Pages 88

The Autobiography of Benjamin Franklin *by Benjamin Franklin*   **ISBN:** *1-59462-135-7*   **$24.95**
The Autobiography of Benjamin Franklin has probably been more extensively read than any other American historical work, and no other book of its kind has had such ups and downs of fortune. Franklin lived for many years in England, where he was agent... Biographies/History Pages 332

Name	
Email	
Telephone	
Address	
City, State ZIP	

☐ **Credit Card**   ☐ **Check / Money Order**

Credit Card Number	
Expiration Date	
Signature	

Please Mail to: Book Jungle
PO Box 2226
Champaign, IL 61825
or Fax to: 630-214-0564

ORDERING INFORMATION

web: *www.bookjungle.com*
email: *sales@bookjungle.com*
fax: *630-214-0564*
mail: *Book Jungle PO Box 2226 Champaign, IL 61825*
or PayPal *to sales@bookjungle.com*

Please contact us for bulk discounts

DIRECT-ORDER TERMS

**20% Discount if You Order
Two or More Books**
Free Domestic Shipping!
Accepted: Master Card, Visa,
Discover, American Express